Canine Cuisine

101 Natural Dog Food & Treat Recipes to Make Your Dog Healthy and Happy

Carlotta Cooper

CANINE CUISINE: 101 NATURAL DOG FOOD & TREAT RECIPES TO MAKE YOUR DOG HEALTHY AND HAPPY

Copyright © 2013 by Atlantic Publishing Group, Inc.
1210 SW 23rd Place • Ocala, Florida 34471
Phone: 800-814-1132–Phone • Fax: 352-622-1875
Website: www.atlantic-pub.com • Email: sales@atlantic-pub.com
SAN Number: 268-1250

Library of Congress Cataloging-in-Publication Data

Cooper, Carlotta, 1962-
 Canine cuisine : 101 natural dog food & treat recipes to make your dog healthy and happy / by Carlotta Cooper.
   p. cm.
 Includes bibliographical references and index.
 ISBN 978-1-60138-399-0 (alk. paper) -- ISBN 1-60138-399-1 (alk. paper) 1. Dogs--Food--Recipes. 2. Dogs--Health. I. Title.
 SF427.4.C67 2012
 636.7'083--dc23
                        2011049400

Printed in the United States

INTERIOR LAYOUT: Antoinette D'Amore • addesign@videotron.ca

Printed on Recycled Paper

A few years back we lost our beloved pet dog Bear, who was not only our best and dearest friend but also the "Vice President of Sunshine" here at Atlantic Publishing. He did not receive a salary but worked tirelessly 24 hours a day to please his parents.

Bear was a rescue dog who turned around and showered myself, my wife, Sherri, his grandparents Jean, Bob, and Nancy, and every person and animal he met (well, maybe not rabbits) with friendship and love. He made a lot of people smile every day.

We wanted you to know a portion of the profits of this book will be donated in Bear's memory to local animal shelters, parks, conservation organizations, and other individuals and nonprofit organizations in need of assistance.

– *Douglas & Sherri Brown*

PS: We have since adopted two more rescue dogs: first Scout, and the following year, Ginger. They were both mixed golden retrievers who needed a home.

Want to help animals and the world? Here are a dozen easy suggestions you and your family can implement today:

- *Adopt and rescue a pet from a local shelter.*
- *Support local and no-kill animal shelters.*
- *Plant a tree to honor someone you love.*
- *Be a developer — put up some birdhouses.*
- *Buy live, potted Christmas trees and replant them.*
- *Make sure you spend time with your animals each day.*
- *Save natural resources by recycling and buying recycled products.*
- *Drink tap water, or filter your own water at home.*
- *Whenever possible, limit your use of or do not use pesticides.*
- *If you eat seafood, make sustainable choices.*
- *Support your local farmers market.*
- *Get outside. Visit a park, volunteer, walk your dog, or ride your bike.*

Five years ago, Atlantic Publishing signed the Green Press Initiative. These guidelines promote environmentally friendly practices, such as using recycled stock and vegetable-based inks, avoiding waste, choosing energy-efficient resources, and promoting a no-pulping policy. We now use 100-percent recycled stock on all our books. The results: in one year, switching to post-consumer recycled stock saved 24 mature trees, 5,000 gallons of water, the equivalent of the total energy used for one home in a year, and the equivalent of the greenhouse gases from one car driven for a year.

Disclaimer

The recipes in this book were collected and are presented to be safe and nutritious for healthy dogs to enjoy. However, you know your dog better than anyone. Only you can know what kinds of food allergies, sensitivities, or medical conditions your dog might have. Please be careful when trying out new foods on your pet. Offer new foods gradually and ensure your pet is able to tolerate them. **Please note that neither the publisher nor the author of these recipes can be held responsible for the dietary needs of your dogs.** *Be sure to consult with your veterinarian if you are unsure. If symptoms are serious, see a vet. Also, monitor your pet for signs of sickness, fatigue, weakness, malnourishment, or obesity. You alone are responsible for using any of the information presented in this book, and any use will be at your own risk.*

Dedication

This book is dedicated to all my dogs who have had to eat my cooking over the years. Thank you for never complaining. I love you all.

Acknowledgments

I would like to thank all of the wonderful owners and breeders who took the time to answer the questionnaire for this book. I would like to especially acknowledge my friend Mari Anderson who has been interested in what to feed dogs and in holistic animal care for a long time and who has taught me a lot. I would also like to thank Magnolia Farm for helping me with some research. Thanks to everyone who helped with the questionnaire and the case studies.

Thanks also to the Greeneville Greene County Public Library and their very kind library staff in Greeneville, Tennessee, for their help with materials.

Thanks to my friend Donna for letting me discuss canine nutrition with her. And, finally, thanks to my terrific dogs, Billie, Blue, Pearl, Brett, and Peyton, for being my taste testers for this book. They let me know which recipes they liked and which ones to toss out. We had a lot of fun.

Table of Contents

Introduction

n 2007, pet owners began to see health problems in their pets; their pets were all showing signs of kidney failure. At first, no one could figure out why pets of all ages that had otherwise been healthy were dying of sudden kidney disease. But a connection was soon made between renal failure in pets and the food they had been eating.

Receiving numerous complaints from customers, Menu Foods in Canada conducted its own in-house testing on some of their pet foods and discovered that some of the animals tested became sick or died. However, the company was unable to determine why the animals were becoming sick. In fact, it took more lab testing by other labs, work by the Food and Drug Administration, and an international investigation leading back to China before they discovered that the ingredient killing cats and dogs was melamine, which is used to make plastic. Melamine, also a cheap protein substitute, had been used in place of wheat gluten and rice protein when these ingredients were produced in China. They were then shipped to importers in the U.S. and on to pet food manufacturers, who had no idea they were putting something harmful in their foods.

There were even fears that melamine had worked its way into the human food supply through contaminated corn gluten and other contaminated vegetable proteins from China. Some contaminated animal feed was fed to pigs later sent to slaughter. It may also have been in fish food fed to farm-raised fish. According to the FDA, up to 3 million people in the United States consumed chicken that had been fed feed contaminated with melamine. These concerns sparked an investigation into protein export contamination in China.

The pet food manufacturers did not know the food they were producing was harmful, so they kept distributing it, and the melamine-contaminated pet food ultimately killed several thousand cats and dogs, according to estimates. Although Menu Foods was the first pet food manufacturer affected by the recalls and the most severely impacted because it made and packaged foods for other companies, virtually every pet food company in North America was affected. Some 5,300 different pet food products were recalled during the crisis, and it was a crisis in North America.

All foods that used wheat gluten and then rice protein were suspect before the specific importer and shipments were identified. There was a panic among owners who did not know what food was safe to feed their pets. The entire pet food industry was severely shaken by the pet food recalls of 2007.

The result of these fears among pet owners was a surge of interest in making homemade pet food. Many owners decided it was safer to make their own food for their dogs.

Concerns About Commercial Pet Foods

Even before the 2007 pet food recalls, there had been growing concerns among pet owners about the ingredients in the foods they were feeding their pets. Ann Martin's alarming 1997 book *Foods Pets Die For: Shocking Facts About Pet Food* asserted that pet food companies used unsavory and even sickening ingredients to make pet foods. She popularized the term the "4 Ds" — referring to the animals used to make pet food as dead, diseased, dying, or decayed. She even asserted that some manufacturers used dead pets to make pet foods. Pet food manufacturers denied her claims in most cases, but her book, and several others like it, made an impact on consumer confidence. It also helped spur the development of companies that use more wholesome ingredients and production practices. By the year 2016, it is now predicted that consumers will spend more on "natural" pet foods than other commercial pet foods, according to the American Pet Products Association, as pet owners try to feed their pets healthier diets.

Making Your Own Pet Food

According to sources such as Pet Nutrition News from **www.PetfoodIndustry.com**, trends in pet food have been following human food trends for some years. Just as people have become more interested in eating healthful diets, they also want their dogs to eat a healthier diet. They like the idea of feeding their dogs organic foods, foods that have less processing, free-range meats, and foods that are, in many cases, locally grown. Many people like their dogs to eat the same kind of healthy foods and get the same good nutrition they get.

Dogs do not need to eat exactly the same kind of diet or foods humans eat, however. Dogs are carnivores, though they can eat like scavengers and benefit from different foods, while humans are omnivores. But dogs can benefit from eating a diet based on a similar healthy philosophy. So, while a vegan diet is not usually a good idea for a dog, your dog can benefit from eating homemade food made from organic foods and fewer processed ingredients. Of course, dogs do not need and will not benefit from every new fad found at your local health store. If you read dog food labels, you will often see companies adding ingredients that are currently popular among human health aficionados even though they will not be any help to a dog. Dog food companies also go through lots of fad diets with their foods. When you make your own homemade food for your dog, you do not have to follow these trends.

People who feed a homemade diet to their dogs often point with pride to their dogs' good condition, shiny coats, good teeth, overall good health, and longevity. Plus, you have the satisfaction and peace of mind of knowing exactly what your dog is eating and that you prepared it. You never have to worry about pet food recalls or the quality of the ingredients you are feeding your dog.

The benefits of making your own pet food

When you buy commercial dog food, no matter how good the quality, you often do not know where the ingredients come from. You do not control how the food is made. You cannot see the quality of the ingredients that go into your dog's food.

When you make your dog's food yourself, you have control over what your dog is eating. You choose each ingredient. You source the ingredients, so if you want your dog to have organic meats, you can buy them. You prepare the ingredients yourself so you know exactly how the food is made. You can choose the best quality ingredients. You can use "human grade" ingredients if you prefer. You can be assured there are no chemicals in your dog's food that could be harmful. Many pet food companies have their own testing in place now to make sure there is no melamine or other contaminants in the ingredients they source from overseas, but this is something you do not need to worry about when you make your own food for your dog.

If your dog has allergies, you can make sure the food does not contain anything that could cause a reaction. If your dog has other special dietary needs, you can ensure he does not have something he should not eat.

There are other reasons for making homemade dog food and treats, of course. Food treats are used more than ever in dog training, especially with positive reinforcement and clicker training, which depend on frequent rewards. Many people like to make homemade treats, cakes, and cookies for their dogs. Homemade treats also make wonderful gifts if you have a friend who is a dog lover. And, in some cases, owners have allergies to certain kinds of dog food. They may need to feed their dogs homemade dog food in order to avoid coming in contact with foods that contain specific allergens.

In addition, most dogs fed with a homemade diet love the food their owner provides. It is not only nutritious but it tastes better than dry kibble from a bag.

In This Book

This book is intended to cover everything you need to know about making your own food for your dog. Chapter 1 will cover commercial dog foods, the good and the bad. It is not all bad. There are some good dog foods available, but it is not always easy to find them. You should know how to judge dog foods, how to read labels, and how to know what ingredients are good for your dog. Once you know more about commercial dog foods, you will know why it is often a better option to cook for your dog. Chapter 2 will discuss homemade diets for dogs and some of the pros and cons. Making your dog's food is a great choice, but it is not always the easiest or fastest thing to do. This chapter will tell you what is involved, what kind of time it takes, how much it might cost, and what tools and appliances you might need. Chapter 3 will look at dog nutrition. If you intend to cook for your dog, you need to know about your dog's nutritional needs. Do not worry. It is not as hard as you think.

Chapter 4 will provide some tips on getting started, such as making sure your dog is in good shape and talking to your vet. Chapter 5 will offer Basic Mealtime Recipes, and Chapter 6 will give recipes for dogs with special conditions. Chapter 7 will discuss portion size and how to know how much to feed your dog. This will help you keep your dog at the right weight and in good health and condition. Chapter 8 will provide recipes for special occasions in case you would like to make a birthday cake or celebrate another occasion with your dog. Dogs like to party, too! Chapter 9 will give information on food storage, traveling with homemade pet food, and food safety tips. Chapter 10 will provide a wrap-up for the book by discussing your homemade diet and what to do if you cannot feed a homemade diet full-time.

A Word From The Author

This book is written as a labor of love. I have been writing about canine nutrition and pet food for years. I have made a homemade diet for some of my senior dogs, for dogs who had allergies, and for puppies going back to the 1980s. I have done my best here to provide you with the most accurate information I have been able to gather. My own dogs have tried and enjoyed many of the recipes in this book. It is my hope that this book will be a great help to you and your dogs and that they will love the meals you cook.

Chapter 1

Facts About Commercial Dog Food

his chapter will examine commercial dog food. Many people begin to consider feeding their dog a homemade diet because they are dissatisfied with commercial pet foods, but not all dog foods are bad. There are some good commercial dog foods, but there are also some low-quality foods. The problem is that it is not always easy to tell the difference. Advertising, companies with well-known brand names, and even some smaller companies who trade on the trend toward "natural" foods can all mislead pet owners into purchasing foods that are not good for their pets. This chapter will look at the beginnings of commercial dog food, where the industry is today, and what makes a healthy dog food. The chapter will also include a listing of some of the best commercial dog foods being made today, in case you cannot cook for your dog.

Dog Food — A History

In some ways, dog food has come a long way in the last 150 years. In the 19th century, and earlier, people typically fed their beloved pet dogs the leavings from their tables. That might not sound desirable, but people did not eat the kind of processed foods we take for granted today, and neither did dogs. Working dogs — farm dogs and hunting dogs — often had a less selective diet unless their owners greatly prized them. Most dogs received bread soaked in water or milk. They only occasionally got meat. When they did get meat, it was offal — the internal organs of butchered animals, and probably not the desirable ones either, such as liver. Offal may sound objectionable to us today, but it is actually healthy and dogs love it, so this was a moderately healthy diet, if somewhat occasional in nature. We often attribute the fact that our dogs are living longer today to improved veterinary care, but better diets probably have a great deal to do with it, too.

The story was somewhat different for carefully raised dogs, and in Victorian times, more and more dogs were being carefully raised. According to one dog writer, writing in 1911, "a dog becomes all the wiser if fed from off his master's plate." Good hunting dogs, for example, were fed the same food as the humans in their household, according to A.F. Hochwalt. Food for raising puppies and young dogs included a mixture of milk, oatmeal porridge, and raw eggs. Cooked and raw lean beef and rib bones were added as puppies got old enough to eat solid food. Hot soup made with carrots, potatoes, and other vegetables could be added to the mixture when the puppies were older. This meal was recommended three times per day for growing puppies. People believed meat was good for dogs, and dogs were receiving meat cuts directly from the same sources as their masters. In actuality, this diet was not so different from the food fed by people who feed a raw diet or who homecook for their dogs today.

It wasn't until the 1860s that someone realized dogs might benefit from more standardized feeding practices. American James Spratt came up with the idea for dog biscuits when he was in London trying to sell, of all things, lightning rods. According to the Pet Food Institute **www.petfoodinstitute. org**, Spratt was offered some discarded ship biscuits for his dog and felt that they were not good enough to feed his companion. This prompted him to invent his own kind of "dog cakes." These first dog biscuits consisted of wheat meals, vegetables, beetroot, and meat. Thus, Spratt became the first maker of pet foods. Spratt's dog cakes were followed later in the U.S., by the company that produced Milk-Bone. This was the limit of "dog food" until around 1922. At this point Ken-L-Ration came on the scene, with its links to the meat packing industry and horse meat. They sold the first canned dog food. Although dogs loved the food, Ken-L-Ration periodically ran into great resistance from American dog owners who disliked the idea of buying horse meat. They achieved more success later when they began to produce dry dog food to compete with Gaines, which had pioneered selling dry dog meal in 1925.

According to the Pet Food Institute:

"When Milk-Bone was acquired by National Biscuits Co. [NaBisCo or Nabisco] in 1931, the idea of using commercially prepared dog foods was still very much ahead of its time. Most dog foods were basically made from waste products, and people were reluctant to spend money on food for their dogs. The knowledge that dogs, as well as people, had nutritional needs which must be satisfied was by no means wide spread...ingredients of the '30s were meat, meat by-products, soybean meal, barley, rice, bran, green bone, vegetables, cod liver oil and charcoal."

Dog food today

The history of pet food in the U.S. since these early days has been one of massive growth as more and more people have added dogs to their families. Pet owners in the U.S. will spend an estimated $19.53 billion on pet food in 2011, according to the American Pet Products Association. People are more concerned, and more aware, than ever before about the health and welfare of their pets. The pet food industry has been incredibly successful at analyzing consumers and their spending habits, as well as playing on their love for their pets, in order to urge them to spend more for dog food. Unfortunately, pet food manufacturers have also been successful at remaining self-regulated. Even the ingredients in dog foods, for the most part, undergo only voluntary inspections. Ingredients imported from other countries, such as wheat gluten meal from China, have in the recent past entered the country without being inspected by the Food and Drug Administration. This is because China exports more products every year and, in the U.S., FDA inspectors have steadily been cut for budgetary reasons since 2001. It is impossible for FDA inspectors to do more than examine a tiny percentage of the products imported into the country. The FDA can only inspect about 89,000 of the imported food shipments that enter the country in any year, out of nearly 9 million. Those figures are from 2007 when there was increased scrutiny of products from China because of the pet food recalls. Products imported from China and elsewhere increase every year.

The USDA, too, which inspects things like meat products, cannot inspect every slaughterhouse in the United States or every facility that manufactures dog food. At a congressional hearing on the pet food recalls in 2007, officials stated that they were satisfied if they could inspect facilities once every three to five years.

In light of these facts, consumers cannot depend upon government agencies to guarantee the safety of the food they feed to their pets. This is a disturbing fact, but it seems an inescapable conclusion. The pet food recalls may be over for now, but it seems only a matter of time before other recalls happen.

What can you, as someone who loves your dog, do to ensure his health? Some people feed a raw diet. Some people cook for their dogs. Or you can purchase good quality commercial dog foods; it just takes a lot of research to find them.

What's in Your Dog's Food?

In 2011, pet food sales in the U.S. will total over $19 billion. As with any large industry that sells millions of products, there is a range of quality in the marketplace.

If you intend to feed your dog a commercial pet food, and that is a viable option, you need to become aware that there is an enormous range of quality among foods. Despite the warm and fuzzy ads, the pretty packaging, and the talking dogs in commercials, remember that dog food companies are businesses. Like other businesses, they have bottom lines. That means that many companies will try to buy the cheapest ingredients possible and sell them for as much as they can get you, the consumer, to pay. This is how melamine ended up in millions of pounds of pet food in 2007. Chinese manufacturers tried to stretch wheat gluten meal, a source of protein in lots of dog food, by adding melamine — a cheap "filler," something used to make plastic but that still qualifies as protein despite its toxic properties. The wheat gluten meal with melamine added qualified as protein when the product was tested for protein percentages in China before export; it was only when the pet food was later tested for added chemicals that the melamine was identified.

American pet food manufacturers range between those companies that consistently use the poorest quality ingredients — usually marked by foods with few named protein sources — to companies somewhere in the middle that have a range of products including low-end foods and higher quality foods, and the higher quality foods that might be hard to find. These foods are usually typified by named protein and fat sources and have fewer added chemicals.

Ingredient quality is the primary difference between foods. It is true that high-quality ingredients will cost more. That seems to be unavoidable. But do not hand over your money without checking out the ingredients. Some dog foods cost more and do not deliver on the quality. You must learn to read the labels and understand what the ingredients mean.

Here is the ingredient list and guaranteed analysis from a high-quality dog food. The food is Orijen Adult Dog Food.

Orijen Adult Dog Food Ingredient List

Fresh boneless chicken, chicken meal, fresh boneless salmon, turkey meal, herring meal, russet potato, peas, sweet potato, fresh boneless turkey, fresh whole eggs, fresh chicken liver, fresh boneless lake whitefish, fresh boneless walleye, sun-cured alfalfa, pea fiber, chicken fat (preserved with mixed tocopherols), organic kelp, pumpkin, chicory root, carrots, spinach, turnip greens, apples, cranberries, blueberries, licorice root, angelica root, fenugreek, marigold flowers, sweet fennel, peppermint leaf, chamomile, dandelion, summer savory, rosemary, vitamin A, vitamin D3, vitamin E, niacin, thiamine mononitrate, riboflavin, d-calcium pantothenate, pyridoxine, folic acid, biotin, vitamin B12, zinc proteinate, iron proteinate, manganese proteinate, copper proteinate, selenium yeast, Lactobacillus acidophilus, Enterococcus faecium.

ORIJEN ADULT DOG FOOD GUARANTEED ANALYSIS	
Crude protein (min.)	38.0 %
Crude fat (min.)	17.0 %
Crude fiber (max.)	3.0 %
Moisture (max.)	10.0 %
Calcium (min./max.)	1.4 % / 1.6 %
Phosphorus (min./max.)	1.2 % / 1.4 %
Omega-6 (min.)	3.0 %
Omega-3 (min.)	1.1 %
DHA (min.)	0.6 %
EPA (min.)	0.3 %
AA (min.)	0.16 %
Carbohydrate (max.)	25%
Ash (max.)	7.5%
Taurine (min.)	0.35 %
Glucosamine (min.)	1400 mg/kg
Chondroitin (min.)	1000 mg/kg
Microorganisms (min.)	120M cfu/kg
pH	5.5

BOTANICAL INCLUSIONS	
Chicory root	700 mg/kg
Licorice root	500 mg/kg
Angelica root	350 mg/kg
Fenugreek	350 mg/kg
Marigold flowers	350 mg/kg
Sweet fennel	350 mg/kg
Peppermint leaf	300 mg/kg
Chamomile flowers	300 mg/kg
Dandelion root	150 mg/kg
Summer savory	150 mg/kg
VITAMINS	
Vitamin A	15 kIU/kg
Vitamin D3	2 kIU/kg
Vitamin E	400 IU/kg
Vitamin B1	0.9 mg/kg
Vitamin B12	0.5 mg/kg
Thiamine	50mg/kg
Riboflavin	45 mg/kg
Niacin	450 mg/kg
Pan. Acid (B5)	50 mg/kg
Pyridoxine (B6)	38 mg/kg
Biotin	1 mg/kg
Folic Acid	5.2 mg/kg
Choline	2700 mg/kg
Ascorbic Acid	55 mg/kg
Beta Carotene	0.44 mg/kg
AMINO ACIDS	
Taurine	0.3%
Lysine	2.45%
Tryptophan	0.38%
Threonine	1.5%
Tyrosine	0.98%

Methionine	0.8%
Isoleucine	1.5%
Leucine	2.9%
Valine	1.85%
Arginine	2.2%
Phenylalanine	1.6%
Histidine	0.8%
Cystine	0.35%
Glutamic Acid	
MINERALS	
Sodium	0.4%
Chloride	0.64%
Potassium	0.77%
Magnesium	0.1%
Sulphur	0.4%
Manganese	27 mg/kg
Cobalt	0.47 mg/kg
Selenium	0.9 mg/kg
Iron	240 mg/kg
Zinc	200 mg/kg
Copper	26 mg/kg
Iodine	0.18 mg/kg

This food is considered by many to be the best dry dog food manufactured today. It contains 80 percent meat (the first five ingredients are meat or fish proteins), and it is grain-free. Other ingredients that make it stand out are named sources of fat (chicken fat), natural preservatives (rosemary, vitamin E), digestive enzymes (lactobacillus acidophilus), and a wide selection of vegetables, fruits, and botanicals. There are no artificial colors, sweeteners, or preservatives. This is an excellent food for an active dog. It is 38 percent protein and 17 percent fat, with omega 3, omega 6, taurine, and glucosamine and chondroitin in the food. Omega 3 and omega 6 are essential fatty acids that are good for your dog's skin and coat, among other things.

Taurine is believed to be good for your dog's heart. Glucosamine and chondroitin are often given to dogs for joint and arthritis issues.

Lower quality commercial dog foods make up the overwhelming majority of foods on the market. These foods commonly stock grocery store shelves and even the pet superstores.

Corn and other grains

How can you tell if a food is a lower quality? It is not that hard. Often, the primary ingredients in these foods will be corn, in one form or another, or other grains. Dogs are carnivores and need protein to thrive. When you see pet foods that rely heavily on grain products, that is a good sign the foods do not provide the kind of quality protein your dog needs. When you look at the guaranteed analysis on the packaging, it might say that the product is 22 percent (or more) protein, but, as we have mentioned with melamine, protein can be made from many things. Not all protein is created equal. Corn can provide protein, but your dog's digestive system is only able to absorb about 54 percent of the protein in corn. Dogs are able to absorb protein from animal sources much more efficiently than from plant sources. However, corn is much cheaper than chicken or lamb, so many dog food companies choose to use corn gluten meal and/or other corn products in their foods as sources of protein. Lots of corn in a food is a sign that the food may be lacking in quality.

Many foods in between low quality and top quality foods may have some amount of corn in them. It will be up to you to decide if you want to include any of these foods in your pet's diet. The presence of corn in a food does not automatically mean that a food is "bad." There are some good foods that do use some corn, in moderation. As energy prices rise, foods with corn in them are also increasing in price or manufacturers are reformulating their recipes to include soy products instead of corn. Corn is not only used in pet foods. It is also used to feed dairy cows (for milk) and to feed cattle (for beef). And, it is used for ethanol in your vehicle. So, corn is in high demand right now. The result has been higher pet food prices. Manufacturers have also been making the size of pet food packaging smaller, so people are paying more for smaller bags of food, as well as changing formulas.

Concerning corn products in dog food, corn is such a commonly used ingredient that many dogs have developed allergies to it. That is one reason why some owners seek out higher quality foods in the beginning, to avoid corn. If you have been feeding your dog a food that is now using soy products, be careful. Soy can also cause upset stomachs because your dog might have problems digesting soy. It is still a vegetable source of protein and not as good as meat protein for your dog, though even some respected dog food companies have been putting soy in their products as a way to increase protein percentages. That is why you should always read the label on your dog's food. Know what is in the food.

"Splitting" is another practice sometimes found in lower quality foods. It refers to the practice of including an ingredient in multiple forms, usually to make it appear that the ingredient is not the largest, or one of the largest ingredients in the food. This is often done in the case of corn. Pet foods are required by law to list their ingredients by descending order of weight before cooking. This means that the company has to list the ingredients that make up the bulk of the food first. So, if whole chicken is listed as the first ingredient, you know that there is more chicken in the food than any other ingredient (although, this is based on weight *before* cooking, so whole chicken will lose water weight during cooking). If ground yellow corn is listed as the first ingredient in the food, that means there is more ground yellow corn in the food than any other ingredient, and that is a bad sign. Pet food companies that engage in the practice of "splitting" will divide up the corn ration in the food so you might see ground yellow corn, corn gluten meal, whole yellow corn, and other forms of corn in the same product. It is all corn, but it is disguised in different forms in the hope that the consumer will not notice it. But your dog's gastrointestinal tract will still know it is corn, and your dog will not digest it better in any form.

Again, corn is not a bad ingredient, and it is present in some good dog foods, but some pet food companies also use it as a less expensive form of protein instead of using meat protein. And some dogs are allergic to corn. So, do check dog food labels to see how much corn is present, especially if your dog has trouble digesting it.

Ideally, if your dog does not have allergies, you would want to see two to three meat proteins in the first five ingredients of a good dog food. For dogs with allergies, focus on one meat protein you know your dog can safely eat. It is not usually a good sign to see corn or other grains as the first or second ingredients in your dog's food.

Byproducts

There are other problems with lower quality dog foods besides the use of corn. The meat sources used are usually less than desirable. One product you will see on ingredient lists is the nonspecific "meat byproducts" as a source of protein. This might sound acceptable to you if you do not know what it is. However, according to the Association of American Feed Control Officials (AAFCO), which suggests guidelines for labeling animal feeds, this is the definition of a meat byproduct:

"the nonrendered, clean parts of slaughtered mammals *other than the meat*."

That is right. Acceptable meat byproducts can include animal lungs, spleens, kidneys, brains, livers, blood, bones, low-temperature fatty tissue, and stomachs and intestines freed of their contents. So, dog foods with "meat by-products" are not the meaty parts of an animal. Moreover, they can be from any animal source, including animals picked up by dead stock removal companies, such as dead zoo animals and large road kill. You have no idea what animal you are feeding to your dog. The byproducts are from mystery meat.

The same is true of the fat in these lower-quality foods. Dogs *do* need fat in order to help absorb fat-soluble vitamins and minerals. But they need good sources of fat, which come from named sources, such as chicken fat. "Animal fat," which you often see listed on the lower quality foods, can be from any animal from the rendering plant. It could be from road kill.

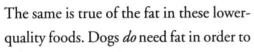

Use *Your* Best Judgment — Not Your Dog's

You cannot trust your dog's judgment on the subject of which food to buy when it comes to meat byproducts and animal fat. Dogs are often quite happy to eat food that is made from lungs, spleens, kidneys, brains, stomachs, and intestines, and they do not care about the animal that was the source. Nor do they care about the source of the animal fat in their food. If you have a dog who has a good appetite, then your dog will likely enjoy eating most kinds of food you put in front of him, regardless of the quality. In addition, many dogs will eat voraciously when you introduce them to a new food, whether it is a good food or not. Foods that are smelly or that have some extra taste will appeal to your dog, no matter what kind of quality the food is. Dogs have a highly developed sense of smell, but their taste buds are far less developed than human taste buds. They do not taste all of the things we taste. If you plan to feed your dog a commercial dog food, choose the food based on quality and not based on what your dog thinks is a good food. It is always good when your dog likes his food and eats it enthusiastically, but the food needs to be nutritious, too.

As mentioned earlier, many of these lower quality foods will be packaged and marketed to compete with higher quality foods. Others are clearly the downscale versions of some of the better foods produced by the big companies. And still others are marketed toward owners who may not be able to afford any other foods for their dogs. But, if you look at the ingredients, these foods will have much in common. Check your grocery store aisle, and you will find many of these foods.

You need to watch out for these same ingredients when you are shopping in pet superstores and looking at foods sold in veterinary offices. You may think that if a food is being sold at a pet superstore or a boutique that it is higher quality, or if a vet touts it that it must be good for your dog, but that is not necessarily the truth. Pet stores carry a wide range of dog foods, and some are better quality than others, regardless of price. Veterinarians receive incentives for selling some foods through their offices, so their food recommendations can be questionable. Look at the ingredients before buying a food, no matter where you are purchasing.

Slaughterhouses, Rendering, and the "4 Ds"

The term "rendering" has come to have bad connotations if you search for information about how dog food is made on the Internet, but it is simply part of the dog food-making process. Basically, rendering removes the fat and water from the meats used in animal feeds. Virtually all commercial dog foods use a similar rendering process because it is necessary to reduce fat and water from the meats. It can be compared, in kitchen terms, to cooking down your meat until only the most essential ingredients are left. Those ingredients are then used to make pet food.

However, what has spurred the negative reputations of rendering plants is that some rendering plants reportedly accept leftover animal parts from animals killed at slaughterhouses, as well as animals picked up by dead stock removal companies. According to the controversial book, *Food Pets Die For*, by Ann Martin, these dead stock removal companies pick up dead animals from zoos, large road kill, restaurant and grocery store garbage (including Styrofoam trays and plastic wrap), and a multitude of euthanized cats and dogs from animal shelters and vet offices. Martin firmly believes that euthanized pets are added to pet food as "meat byproducts" in the lower quality foods. Pet food manufacturers dispute the allegation that dead pets are included in pet food in any form.

It should be said that Martin is an avid animal rights activist, and she is a harsh critic of the pet food industry. Her information about the rendering process and how dog food is made is accurate, but the information is presented with a great deal of bias. Not all of her allegations against the pet food industry can be substantiated. However, Martin has had an enormous impact on other people writing about pet food. Most of the books and Internet sites that discuss pet foods rely on Martin as a source.

Higher quality dog food companies claim to use rendered animals and parts that come from better sources. Depending on the company, they may use animals that are organically raised, free-range chickens, pasture-raised animals, grass-fed beef, and parts that are "human grade," although pet food is not allowed to be advertised as "human grade" by law. There are some questions about whether all companies that make these claims are believable or not. No doubt many companies are being truthful. However, it was discovered during the 2007 pet food recalls that some companies that made these claims were having their foods made and packaged by Menu Foods, using the same formulas as Menu's other, lesser quality clients, and using the same machinery in the same plants.

If you are buying a dog food that makes such claims — and charges more for them — it is good to do some research into their claims to make sure they have a good reputation and that they can substantiate their ingredient claims. It is even better if they have their own dog food plant and make their own food. Dog food companies do not usually render their own foods and instead leave that job to rendering plants that can deal in large volumes of animal material, some of it intended for the human food market in the form of lard made from animal fat. However, after receiving baked down dry matter from the rendering plant, some pet food manufacturers do have their own facilities where the food is mixed according to their proprietary recipes. At least then you know that the company is not using some other dog food company's formula or ingredients. Unfortunately, some dog food companies refuse to give out this kind of information and will not tell you where the food is made. This is usually a bad sign. It often means that another company is manufacturing their food for them.

The rendering process — the good and the bad

Before slaughterhouses ship any animal parts to the renderers, animal parts are "denatured." That means that they are sprayed with one of several toxic denaturing products to help break the meats down during the rendering process using enzymes. These products are technically "poisons," and they are freely applied to all parts of the carcasses sent to the renderers. According to some people, these denaturing products are also applied to the meats to prevent the pet food from re-entering the human food market. Critics allege that these toxins become part of the pet food and may be harmful to your pet or even cause cancer. Some better quality dog foods do not use denaturing products on their animal ingredients. They are usually the foods that claim to use "human grade" ingredients. If you are interested in purchasing dog food that is made without denaturing products, contact your dog food company and ask them if they use these products.

At the rendering plant, a machine grinds the parts in vats, and the mixture is cooked at 280 degrees F for one hour. The mixture is spun at high speed, and the grease (tallow) rises and is removed. This fat becomes the source of much of the generic fat you find in pet foods. After the grease is removed, the mixture is cooked and dried in several steps and moved along a large pipeline until it is dry enough to come out as meat meal and meat and bone meal. According to AAFCO, meat meal is "the rendered product from mammal tissues, exclusive of blood, hair, hoof, horn, hide trimmings, manure, stomach and rumen contents except in such amounts as may occur unavoidably in good processing practices." Meat and bone meal is slightly different. According to AAFCO it is "the rendered product from mammal tissues, including bone, exclusive of blood, hair, hoof, horn, hide trimmings, manure, stomach and rumen contents, except in such amounts as may occur unavoidably in good processing practices." Once these ingredients are dry, they can then be used in pet food as "meat byproduct."

Besides fat rendered from animal bodies during the rendering process, other sources of fat in your dog's food can come from oil and grease from restaurants. Remember that named sources of fat are better when you are looking at a dog food label, such as chicken fat. You will not be able to tell that the vegetable oil or animal fat in your dog's food came from a restaurant. Many dog food processing plants have arrangements with local businesses such as restaurants. If a dog food plant is near a poultry processor, then it is not unusual for them to get their chicken parts from that processor. The same is true if there is a beef slaughterhouse nearby. This saves the company money and the animal parts are fresher.

As Martin graphically describes, the lower quality rendering plants depend upon the "4 Ds" — dead, dying, diseased, and disabled animals. According to Martin, there is nothing to prevent the stock removal companies from accepting animals that have died of disease or that are disabled or dying of old age or other ailments. These animals are included in the rendering vats along with the miscellaneous carcasses from the slaughterhouses. This is why meat meal, meat "byproducts," and other unnamed meat sources are not a good nutritional source for your pet. The heating process during rendering might kill overt disease, but such sources offer little quality nutrition.

Other concerns come from the fact that animals that die on farms may take days to reach the slaughterhouse. Dead animals are contaminated with countless bacteria that go into the vats, and animals raised for food receive numerous antibiotics and medications that also go into our pets' food supply. However, the USDA does have required withdrawal periods for animals sent to slaughter, and animals cannot receive antibiotics or certain medications within a specified time prior to slaughter to supposedly allow time for the chemicals to leave their system. This is true for animals in the human food chain as well.

Although Martin's work in 1997 was the original book to examine the issue of how pet food is made and the possible problems in the industry, there have been a number of other authors since that time which have taken a look at the same subject and drawn similar conclusions. In *What's Really In*

Pet Food, the Animal Protection Institute (an animal rights organization) notes that much larger international food corporations own most pet food companies. This allows these food corporations to funnel waste from their other food-making companies into their pet food businesses. It is a win-win situation for these corporations. They can use the better meat parts for the human foods they make, for example, and then use the less desirable parts to make pet foods. Some of the large food corporations and their pet food subsidiaries include:

Nestlé (Alpo, Fancy Feast, Friskies, Mighty Dog, and Ralston Purina products such as Dog Chow, ProPlan, and Purina One); Heinz (9 Lives, Amore, Gravy Train, Kibbles-n-Bits, Nature's Recipe); Colgate-Palmolive (Hill's Science Diet Pet Food). Other leading companies include Procter & Gamble (Eukanuba and Iams; recently purchased Natura, California Natural, EVO, HealthWise, Innova, and Karma Organic); Mars (Kal Kan, Mealtime, Pedigree, Sheba, Waltham's); and Nutro. Nestle, Mars, Proctor & Gamble, and Colgate-Palmolive control about 80 percent of the pet food market in the entire world.

Dr. Wendell O. Belfield, DVM, in *Food Not Fit For A Pet*, agrees with Martin that American pets were being used as part of the rendering process, at least in the early 1980s. Dr. Belfield was a meat inspector for the USDA and the State of California, and he is quite critical of the pet food industry. There are other, similar articles such as *A Look Inside a Rendering Plant*, by Gar Smith, *The Dark Side of Recycling* (anonymous), and *Concerns about Commercial Pet Food*, by William Pollak, DVM.

None of this information is meant to particularly discourage you from using the better commercial dog foods to feed your dog. The government simply has different standards for what is allowed in pet food and what is allowed in human food. Remember that there are some good commercial dog foods that exceed these standards. However, this information just serves to illustrate the amount of unknown, mysterious, or even dangerous ingredients that could be present in your dog's food.

Although unsavory components can go into meat meal and meat byproducts, the slaughterhouse and rendering process are similar for all kinds of meats used in making pet food. Dog foods of all qualities go through the rendering process. There are also beef byproducts, chicken byproducts, and so on. These are better ingredients than the unnamed "meat" byproducts because at least you know what animal the parts are from, but they are not the best parts of the animal. Chicken byproducts are not as good as whole chicken or chicken meal; they include the head, feet, entrails, lungs, spleen, kidneys, brain, liver, stomach, bones, blood, or intestines. Just because a product claims to be made from chicken or some other protein source does not mean it is good for your dog.

Keep in mind that quality dog food is generally made the same way as other dog foods with few exceptions. The process is the same. Only the ingredients will be different. There are a few dog foods that are oven-baked instead of pushed out by an extruder and cut into small nuggets, the way most dog food is made, for example. (An extruder is like a Play-Doh factory — it pushes the dog food "dough" through so it can come out and be cut in various small shapes.) Flint River Ranch is a good dog food that sells oven-baked food. Their food is advertised as "human grade."

Commercial Dog Foods and Your Dog's Needs

Commercial dog foods today are regulated by the Food and Drug Administration (FDA), by the Association of American Feed Control Officials, and by state regulatory agencies. They are also self-regulated, though that does not always make consumers feel confident.

These organizations monitor the labeling on pet foods, require ingredients to be listed, and require a guaranteed analysis of the food's protein, fat, and other nutrients. The United States Department of Agriculture does a certain amount of inspection at pet food manufacturing plants and slaughterhouses and of other ingredients used in pet foods. However, in reality, only a small percentage of the meat and other contents used in pet foods is actually inspected. The guaranteed analysis on a pet food label can even be misleading. A food may say it contains 22 percent protein, but that does not indicate the quality of the protein, or how digestible it will be for your dog. The protein may come from an animal's hooves, for instance, or bird beaks in some foods. That protein is not the same quality as 22 percent protein from a food that obtains meat from chicken meal or lamb meal.

You should also beware some labeling quagmires when you buy dog food. According to the Food and Drug Administration, there are a few rules that can make buying dog food particularly difficult when it comes to knowing what is in the food. Take the "95 percent rule." If a food is called "Beef for Dogs," then it has to be 95 percent beef. However, if it is called "Dog Food with Beef," it only has to be 3 percent beef. That is the 3 percent rule. Then there is the 25 percent rule. This is also called the "dinner" rule. If the product is called "Beef Dinner for Dogs" or "Beef Formula for Dogs" then it only has to contain 25 percent beef. The other 75 percent of the food only has to meet the minimum standards for dog food. It does not have to be meat at all. These rules are particularly important for people who buy canned dog food and for people whose dogs have allergies. They may think they are buying a product that is mostly one kind of meat, only to discover that half the food is some meat their dogs are allergic to.

Holistic and organic

Top quality dog food manufacturers have exploded on the scene in the last ten to 15 years as people have become more aware of the ingredients in pet foods and holistic foods in general. Some of the manufacturers, such as Old Mother Hubbard, have been around for a long time, but it has only been in the last few years that sales of super premium pet foods have really taken off. Old Mother Hubbard, famous for their natural snacks and dog biscuits, is now owned by WellPet, the same company that owns Wellness and Eagle Pack, as well as Holistic Select. All of these companies are well known and highly respected for making good dog foods.

According to the Organic Trade Association, organic pet food sales grew at a rate of 48 percent in 2008. Sales totaled $84 million in 2009. Sales have increased by a factor of ten since 2002. Organic pet food sales represented the fastest growing non-food category among organic sales in the U.S. Pet food sales are considered "non-food" because they are not human food.

The term "holistic" is somewhat suspect when it comes to pet food, and so is the term "natural." The Food and Drug Administration has no formal definitions for these terms, which has led to many pet food companies tossing them around rather indiscriminately on pet food labels. These terms often entice consumers to buy products because they believe the dog food is healthier for their pets without any real proof that it is. Pet foods that call themselves "holistic" can contain chemicals and meat that are made from byproducts, artificial ingredients, and other less desirable ingredients. Even if a food claims to be "natural" or "holistic," read the ingredients to see what the food contains.

However, the term "organic" is a legitimate term, and it does have a specific meaning when it appears on a pet food label. If a pet food claims to be organic or to use organic ingredients, you can take that claim seriously and give it some weight. "Organic" or "certified organic" means that the food and the way it has been produced on the farm have met certain government inspection criteria.

Two quality organic foods are Castor & Pollux and Newman's Own. These companies have dog foods that are 70 to 94 percent organic. Some Newman's Own dog foods are 95 percent organic, according to their website. Foods that are 70 to 94 percent organic mean that most of their ingredients are organic. The ingredients come from farms that have been organically certified. This means that the animals and vegetables are raised without chemicals. Natural methods are used, and the animals are fed foods that do not contain certain additives such as growth hormones or arsenic. Certifying organizations inspect the farms to make sure the regulations to maintain organic status are followed. There are not many dog foods that are truly organic, though some claim to have organic ingredients. These two foods stand out.

Manufacturers of better quality foods are described as "conscientious" and concerned about the health of pets, and that is one of their selling points. It shows in the ingredients they use in their foods, which include named meats such as chicken and lamb and often more exotic meats such as venison, duck, salmon, and others. Many foods use grains other than corn, such as whole grain rice, or starches such as potatoes or sweet potatoes. Some foods have turned away from grains altogether and have argued that from a nutritional standpoint dogs do not need the carbohydrates offered by grains. Fats are also from named sources. Some foods pride themselves on offering single-sources of protein and fewer ingredients — good for dogs with allergies.

All of these attributes are signs of better foods, and they are undertaken as part of these companies' voluntary higher standards. Other voluntary higher standards include regular testing for contamination from their production runs, sampling of the product to make sure it is meeting the recipe requirements, visiting production facilities for inspections, and testing of ingredients prior to use to make sure they meet company standards. All of these procedures can give added assurance to the consumer that the dog food is of the high quality claimed by the manufacturer. Because many of the companies making "holistic" or natural dog foods are not well known by the general public, company reputation for quality in manufacturing among dog owners has come to be important for their sales. A recall or a reputation for poor customer service can seriously harm a small company that specializes in holistic dog food.

The companies making better quality foods usually sell their foods through individual dealers or on the Internet, though some can be found in pet stores. Prices are typically high, so the consumer must be convinced he or she is getting the best quality food for the money. The foods often use human-grade ingredients, although dog foods cannot by law be labeled "human grade." They do not use meats that were rejected by the human food industry, as some lower quality companies may do. The better quality companies may also use hormone-free and antibiotic-free meats. Some even use free-range and pasture-raised meats. Of course, all poultry in the

United States is hormone-free, but other meat sources may be given hormones unless the food you are feeding stipulates that it is hormone-free.

These better quality companies will make use of higher quality ingredients throughout their formulations. In addition to the ingredients already mentioned, these include using natural preservatives such as vitamin C or E instead of BHA, BHT, or ethoxyquin and no artificial colors, sugars, or sweeteners.

 A Hidden Toxin

Ethoxyquin is problematic in dog foods. It may appear in the ingredient list of some lower quality foods as a preservative. However, even if it is not listed as an ingredient, it may be included in your dog's food. Ethoxyquin is commonly used as a preservative for fish. If it is added to the fish before it reaches the dog food manufacturing plant, then the company is not required to list it on their label. Ethoxyquin is banned for human consumption, except in minute amounts for spices. It is usually used in rubber production. It is not something you want your dog to eat. There are a few companies that state on their websites that they purchase fish that has not been preserved with ethoxyquin. If your dog food does not state this fact, then you can assume the fish in your dog's food has been preserved with ethoxyquin.

Here are a list of dog foods that do not contain fish or fish meal preserved with ethoxyquin at the time of this writing:

Acana (also made by Champion, which makes Orijen)
Blue Buffalo
California Natural
EVO
Wellness

Dogswell

Earthborn Holistic

Taste of the Wild

Castor & Pollux

Flint River Ranch

Healthwise

Innova

Karma

Natura

Orijen

Solid Gold

There may be a few other foods that have fish or fish meal that is not preserved with ethoxyquin. The list fluctuates as companies make decisions about their ingredients and expenses.

Some of the better companies will also include desirable additives such as omega 3 and 6 fatty acids for improved skin and coat; glucosamine and chondroitin for joint health; digestive enzymes to help dogs digest; and antioxidants such as blueberries and other berries. Many better companies today are also adding the amino acid taurine to their foods for good heart health. Taurine has been added to cat food for many years, but it was not added to dog foods because dogs are able to convert carnitine, produced by the liver and kidneys, and make their own taurine. However, it is now thought that a taurine deficien-

cy can lead to dilated cardiomyopathy. If your dog food does not contain taurine, you can add fish oil to your dog's diet and it will supply the necessary taurine.

However, even most of these better foods will contain some ingredients that you might find objectionable. For example, rosemary is often linked to seizures in dogs that are epileptic or prone to seizures. Yet it is used as a natural preservative, and it can be hard to find good dog foods that do not contain this ingredient.

AAFCO

You also want foods that meet Association of American Feed Control Officials (AAFCO) standards that state they provide a complete diet. This is a bare minimum requirement for any food. It does not guarantee that a food is good for your dog, but without at least meeting this standard, your dog would be in severe dietary trouble.

The AAFCO label means that a company has conducted a six-month feeding trial of the food on a minimum number of dogs (eight) and 75 percent of the dogs (six) completed the trial in good health. There is no follow-up to see how the dogs do after the trial. Or, the company can submit data that shows the food meets the minimum nutrient requirements. So, the AAFCO seal is not a ringing endorsement of your dog's food, but it is better than nothing. When in doubt, choose a food that has had the six-month feeding trial.

The dog food label will state whether the food has undergone a food trial or submitted data to meet minimum nutrient requirements. If a food trial has been conducted there will be a statement similar to this: "Animal feeding tests using AAFCO procedures substantiate that (name of product) provides complete and balanced nutrition." If the product is using the minimum nutrient requirements instead, there will be a statement similar to this one: "(Name of product) is formulated to meet the nutritional levels established by the AAFCO Dog Food Nutrient Profiles." The exact wording can vary from one company to another.

At least those foods have actually been fed to real dogs. Even some of the foods produced by the better quality companies might not meet the AAF-CO standard due to the fact they are unbalanced and expect the owner to supplement the food with other products. If you purchase one of these foods, make sure you follow label directions and supplement as directed so your dog has his nutritional needs met. For example, if you buy a meat product that is mostly protein and is designed to be fed with a raw diet, it probably advises you to mix with another product so your dog will get the required vitamins and minerals in his food. If you do not use the recommended mix, your dog will not have his nutritional needs met. Look for the AAFCO statement that the food you are buying is nutritionally complete, or make sure you understand the feeding directions so you are meeting your dog's needs.

The best commercial foods

After reading about the rendering process and how dog food is made, you may be thinking that there are no good dog foods, but that is not the case. There are many good dog food companies making excellent foods.

Often, finding a good food for your dog is complicated by your dog's specific health needs. If your dog has allergies, IBD, diabetes, or kidney problems, for example, then finding a "good" dog food becomes much more difficult, but it can still be done in many cases. You will probably need to work with your veterinarian to determine what your dog is able to eat and what he should avoid before you can select a food. You may also need to work with a canine nutritionist or other specialist.

Keep in mind that there is no "best" dog food. Every dog is different. The best food for your dog may not be the best food for your friend's dog. However, there are foods that meet high standards and which provide excellent nutrition for dogs. Here is a list of foods considered the best commercial foods.

- Acana
- Addiction
- Annamaet
- Artemis
- Back To Basics
- By Nature Organics
- Castor & Pollux Organix
- Chicken Soup for the Pet Lover's Soul
- Drs. Foster & Smith
- Dog Lover's Gold
- Dogswell
- Eagle Pack & Holistic Select (owned by the same company)
- FirstMate
- Flint River Ranch
- Fromm, Four Star Nutritionals, Gold Nutritionals
- Holistic Blend
- Horizon Pet Nutrition
- Natural Planet Organics
- Newman's Own Organics
- Orijen
- Petcurean, Go! Natural

- Solid Gold
- Taste of the Wild
- Timberwolf Organics (not organic)
- VeRUS Pet Foods
- Vets Choice Holistic Health Extension
- Wellness
- Wysong

Many of the foods listed here use human grade, antibiotic-free ingredients. They generally have higher protein percentages than typical dog foods, and they offer grain-free foods for consumers who wish to avoid feeding their dogs grains. You will need to look at specific products to make sure the dog food is the correct choice for your dog. Some foods may not be a good choice for puppies, for instance, that need specific calcium amounts in their diets. Look at protein and fat percentages, especially if your dog has any health issues.

The foods listed here are generally rather expensive. If you have large dogs or if you have multiple dogs, then feeding some of these foods can be difficult for some dog owners. Yet you may still want to provide your dog with good nutrition from a commercial dog food. Here are some good dog foods that are more moderate in price.

- Taste of the Wild (grain-free, High Prairie Canine Formula and others)
- Drs. Foster & Smith Dry Adult Dog Food (Chicken & Brown Rice Formula and others)
- Chicken Soup for the Pet Lover's Soul
- Kirkland Dog Food (Lamb and Rice formula), from Costco
- Purina Pro Plan formulas (Performance, Sensitive Stomach, and others)
- Black Gold (Ultimate Adult)

Some people will criticize some of these foods, but Kirkland Lamb and Rice is an extremely popular food among people who breed and show dogs. The food contains no corn or wheat. Lamb and lamb meal are the first two ingredients.

Many dog food connoisseurs are critical of Purina because some of their grocery store brands are not top quality and contain plenty of corn. However, the Pro Plan formulas are medium- to high-quality foods. Some of them do contain corn and wheat, so if your dog has problems digesting these ingredients, you will need to avoid these foods. Otherwise, the Pro Plan formulas are good foods and most dogs can eat them without any problems. Purina is also a reputable company with good production values. They are rarely involved in pet food recalls, unlike many smaller companies that claim to make organic and "holistic" foods but that are in the news much more often for production problems and issues with salmonella.

Black Gold is a company that is better known among hunters and people with working dogs. They offer a 100 percent refund if you are not satisfied with the food. Their Ultimate Adult formula has no corn, no wheat, no soy, no fillers, no artificial coloring, and no chemical preservatives. Black Gold also conducts feeding trials. However, Black Gold can be hard to find. You can check feed stores and visit their website (**http://blackgolddogfood. com/cornfree.htm**) to find dealers.

On the other hand, you might want to cook for your dog, but you do not have time to do so often. If you live in a large city, then it is possible to find a butcher or dog food shop that can do the cooking for you. According to a recent *New York Times* story about homemade pet food, reported in its Dining & Wine section, butcher shops in Brooklyn and San Francisco that sell "pet food" are doing a booming business. At one store, a custom mix of ground meats, organs, vegetables, garlic, eggs, and other ingredients sells for $3.25 per pound. Marrow bones are also a big seller. They are often bought as treats for dogs. Another store reports that they sell 250 to 300 pounds of beef offal and whole ground chicken per week to satisfy their pet food customers. Many of their customers specifically ask for chicken backs and organs so they can make their own pet food.

The story also mentions a pet store in Manhattan that sells a mixture of cooked turkey or chicken, broccoli, cauliflower, and other vegetables, along with vitamins and minerals, for $8.95 per pound.

These may be options for you to consider if you live in an area that has such businesses. This is not an economical way to feed your dog, but if you would like to cook for your dog and you have little time to cut up food yourself, then this is a way that could work for you, especially if you have a small dog that would not cost too much to feed.

The Bottom Line

Despite all of the warnings and caveats about dog food today, there are many excellent dog foods available to consumers. The important thing for dog owners to learn is that they must read the labels. It is not always easy to tell the good foods from the lesser quality foods, but if you read the labels and understand the ingredients, you can select a good quality food for your dog. Do not be fooled by terms such as "holistic" and "natural" which have no real meaning. The ingredients are what matter.

The next chapter will look at cooking for your dog and why that may be a better choice for you and your canine friend.

Chapter 2

A New Alternative

hapter 1 examined commercial dog food, both its beginnings and its status today. Although there are many lower quality foods that are not as healthy for your dog, it is possible to buy good quality commercial food for your dog, provided you do some research and learn to read pet food labels. If you understand what kind of ingredients are in the food you are considering for your dog and where they are sourced from, then you stand a good chance of finding a good food.

However, for many dog owners today, the nutrition and convenience offered by even the better quality commercial dog foods are not enough. They want the healthiest diet possible for their dogs, and they feel that can only be obtained by formulating and preparing their dogs' diets themselves. In some cases, they might have dogs with allergies or with specific health problems, such as diabetes, that require a special diet. Or, they might have a senior dog or a dog that needs to have his weight monitored carefully to gain or lose pounds. But many people choose to feed their dogs a home-cooked diet simply because they feel it is far superior in terms of nutrition.

The Benefits and Challenges of Making Homemade Food for Your Dog

If you are interested in cooking for your dog, there are many things your dog can get from a homemade diet that he cannot get from commercial dog food. You can make sure you use the best quality ingredients, including better ingredients than your dog would get in even the best commercial dog foods. For some people this means buying organic meats and vegetables for preparation, while others simply like to buy locally grown meat and vegetables. Others are happy just knowing they have selected the ingredients themselves. Making your own food for your dog is not about being judged by someone else or trying to live up to someone else's standards. It is about preparing food for your dog that you are comfortable serving.

Some people assume that cooking for your dog is an expensive proposition. They might have this belief because it often seems that if something is "better," it costs more. However, preparing food at home for your dog does not necessarily have to cost more than buying a good dog food. In fact, there are some ways you can cut costs by using co-op buying schemes with other people who cook for their dogs or by buying in bulk. Plus, there are other things to consider, such as hidden values in homecooking. Having a healthier dog means that you will be making fewer trips to the vet, and that will save you lots of money in the long-run.

When making a homemade diet for your dog, you can control the entire food-making process yourself. You select the ingredients, you prepare them the way you want, and you add whatever "extras" you like to the mix, whether that includes prebiotics, probiotics, supplements, and so on. *Prebiotics, probiotics, supplements, and other things your dog might need in his food will be covered in Chapter 3.* You can choose your own recipes for your dog so he always likes what you feed him. You can make food in small batches so it is always fresh. You can fulfill any particular needs your dog might have, such as allergies or specific health problems. These are some of the tangible benefits to you and your dog from following a homemade diet:

- The satisfaction of knowing your dog is healthier
- Knowing exactly what your dog is eating, and the peace of mind that comes with that knowledge
- Being able to teach your children about caring for a pet, including his diet
- Making a food that is more environmentally friendly

Instead of using a commercial dog food that puts chemicals into the air and water, you are making green food at home. You can even buy locally, if you prefer, which sends a good message to your friends and neighbors, as well as cutting down on the high transportation costs of food in this country. Your local farmers will thank you.

CASE STUDY: HOMECOOKING AFTER THE PET FOOD SCARE
Gilda Ferguson, DDS, PhD

Gilda Ferguson has been home cooking for her two Irish Setters, Jake and Britney, for almost five years. Both are in excellent health and are good eaters. Jake recently was diagnosed as Lyme positive and is doing very well with treatment.

Several years ago, I was feeding what was touted as high-quality kibble and canned food. At the time, I had two rescue Miniature Pinchers and a 4-month-old Irish Setter male puppy. All three began to refuse their food and had bloody diarrhea. The culprit was the melamine that was being used to up the protein content in pet food. The two Min Pins recovered, but the Irish has had a sensitive stomach every since. The Irish, Jake, still cannot drink cold water either without throwing up. We keep his water on a small warmer that maintains a constant warm temperature.

That was when I began to cook for the dogs, as I felt I could no longer trust commercially prepared dog food. At first, I followed a recipe that I found in a magazine that was from Dr. Pitcairn's diet. I have altered that over time as I have learned what my dogs like, and what is good for them. The first recipes were essentially stews that have evolved to the meatloaf mix that I now cook. I find recipes through dog lists, the Internet, magazines, and books.

I currently feed a combination of very high-quality kibble from Acana and my "meatloaf." The basis of the meatloaf consists of various combinations of the following: ground beef, ground turkey, eggs, sweet potatoes, carrots, celery, thyme, rosemary, apples or blueberries, molasses, ketchup, cheese, and barbecue sauce. My ratio is about one-third kibble to two-thirds homecooked. At times, I feed all homecooked with no kibble. My dogs turn their noses up at plain kibble or canned food.

I spend my Saturday afternoons every other weekend purchasing, chopping, and cooking. I would say that is approximately four to five hours. I buy my meat in bulk at Costco. If I don't like the look of the meat, I will go to Walmart and buy in bulk. I buy carrots, apples, and blueberries in bulk from Costco. I use organic food as often as I can find it. The vegetables I use are organic. The spices are not. They are bought in bulk. Eggs are organic and the cage free, free-range type.

I have also found that Jake will warn me when the food is not good. He will look at it, look at me, sit down in front of his bowl, and refuse to eat. I will add that I fed straight homecooked meals after the scare with the pet food. It has only been recently that I've added kibble back to their diets. I also supplement with salmon oil and vitamin C tablets placed on their food.

I would absolutely recommend homecooking. My dogs have no skin problems and no allergies, their eyes are bright and shiny, and they are full of energy. My vet always compliments us on our dogs and their appearance.

I tell others to read as much material as they can lay their hands on. The more you read, the more you learn that most commercial kibble is just horrible. You might as well feed cardboard to your dogs. Once you've read a lot, talk to friends who cook for their dogs, and finally consult your vet. You want to make sure what you cook is nutritious.

The biggest challenges are the expense and the time needed to pre-pare the food. I work full time, and I use a lot of my weekend time to devote to my dog food preparation.

The biggest rewards are watching my dogs sit by the butcher block, waiting for me to defrost and heat up their dinner. Their eyes follow my every move, and their tongues lick their lips. Cleaning up the drool is a pain, though. Then seeing their pleasure in their meal makes me feel really good.

If I could afford it, I would eliminate the kibble completely.

However, there are also some challenges to watch out for when you start to make your own homemade dog food:

- Learning what your dog needs to stay healthy
- Taking the time to buy the ingredients and prepare the meals
- Buying special kitchen equipment for preparation, some of which can be costly

None of these things should be daunting to you. If you can prepare healthy meals for your family, you will be able to prepare healthy meals for your dog. The key to feeding your dog a healthy diet is to provide variety in his meals. If he does not get all of the nutrients he needs in one meal, he will make up for it in the next meal. If you can set aside a few hours each week, then you will have time to prepare a full week's worth of meals for your dog ahead of time. You can then freeze meals and take them out as you need them.

There are also many excellent resources available to help you learn more about dog nutrition. Many good books have been written on the subject, and you will find some of them listed in the Appendix of this book. There are also some good websites online about dog nutrition, as well as email lists and chat groups for people who cook for their dogs. *You can find a listing of some of these mail lists and chat groups in the Appendix.* Joining one of these groups is a good way to make friends with others who cook for their dogs and who have the same interests, successes, and concerns about their dogs and their diets. There is lots of information available about dog nutrition and homecooking. Just be sure you are getting your information from a good source, as not all of what you find is reliable. Check and double-check the information you get about canine nutrition to make sure it is valid before you try something on your dog.

There are a few items of kitchen equipment you might need to get started, such as a meat grinder or a food processor, but you may already have these items. If you do not, they are one-time investments.

The nice thing about making homemade dog food is that you will be using the same cuts of meat and other ingredients for your dog's food as you use for your own family's food. That means that it is perfectly all right to use the same pots and pans and other kitchen items when making your dog's food. You do not have to go out and buy a second set of cookware. Naturally, you will need to follow scrupulous hygiene procedures in the kitchen, but your dog will not be eating out of your cookware. When you cook chicken for your dog, it will not be any different from cooking chicken for yourself. You will simply serve it in your dog's dish.

The next chapter will examine dog nutrition in closer detail. Before you can cook for your dog, you will need to know more about a dog's natural diet and what he needs to be healthy.

Chapter 3

Dog Nutrition

rom their lives as wolves to today, the dog's diet has changed over the millennia. Although they are carnivores and they need meat protein in their diet, the dog is also something of a scavenger, so they can eat many different foods. This chapter will look at how the dog's diet has evolved and how commercial foods do and do not meet their needs. It will also look at the dog's "natural" diet and what dogs need today in order to be healthy.

The Basics of Canine Nutrition

As most people know, dogs descended from wolves. Researchers theorize today, based on DNA findings, that domesticated dogs first developed from wolves in Southeast Asia. These early wolf-dogs may have been attracted to living with humans because of the ease with which they could obtain food. Leftovers and garbage may have first enticed our dog friends to join us. Scavenging through bones and food fragments left by people might have lured these wolves closer to people until the wolves were slowly domesticated.

Our dogs still retain the hallmarks of these canines: carnivores with an ability to scavenge and survive on lots of different kinds of food. Unlike cats, which require a protein diet to survive, dogs are more adaptable and similar to omnivores. This is not to say they thrive on a plant diet or that you can successfully feed them anything at all, but it is one key to their amazing survival skills. For optimum health, however, this chapter will discuss how to best meet their needs.

Protein

The main part of any dog's diet needs to be based on animal protein and animal fats. Unlike humans, dogs get most of their energy requirements from these sources and not from carbohydrates. Most of an animal's body is made up of protein — muscles, skin, blood, and internal organs. Proteins contain essential amino acids, and these must be eaten daily to avoid a protein deficiency.

There are differences in proteins, and some proteins are better for your dog than others because he will be better able to digest them and use their nutritional values. A dog could digest virtually all of an egg's protein. Muscle meats from beef, poultry, bison, and fish are all good sources of protein and are highly digestible. However, other sources of protein can be much less so. That is why package labeling can be so misleading when it comes to dog foods. One dog food's "22 percent protein" can be vastly different from the same percentage of protein in a lower quality food that derives protein from chicken feet and beaks. Your dog will not be able to absorb protein as well from the inferior food, and it will show in his health.

Fats

Contrary to popular opinion, fats are necessary for good health. Fats such as omega-3 fatty acid, omega-6 fatty acid, and arachidonic fatty acid are considered essential fatty acids. They are necessary for cell structures and cell membranes in the body. Some vitamins and minerals are "fat-soluble," which means they are only absorbed with the help of fats or lipids. Otherwise your dog cannot use them. Fats also support the immune system and help blood movement. Again, fats vary in quality depending on their source, just as protein sources do.

Carbs

Carbohydrates are the sugars and starches in your dog's diet. Grains and cereals in dog foods, however, provide carbohydrate energy. It is not necessary to completely eliminate grains from your dog's diet, unless you wish to do so, but avoid foods that have grains as the primary ingredients. Carbohydrates for dogs can serve some useful purposes. In addition to providing energy through glucose and other sugars, carbohydrates provide fiber to help to move food through a dog's intestines. Dogs are not able to digest fiber as completely as humans, and their digestive tract is not as long by comparison, so ingredients that help move food along and prevent fermentation in the gut are helpful. Foods that produce fermentation are prone to producing gas and flatulence in your dog. Dog foods that contain lots of fillers and fibers can cause dogs to produce gas. Culprits include soy products, fruits, peas, beans, and dairy products in dogs that have trouble digesting them.

On the other hand, foods that are too high in carbohydrates and fiber, or with carbohydrates and fiber that are not easily digested, may produce

bloated symptoms in your dog, or actual bloat, which is a life-threatening condition.

Some people do prefer to eliminate carbohydrates from their dog's foods as much as possible for dietary reasons. Be aware that some form of starch is usually required in kibbled foods in order for the dry food to retain a dough consistency for the sake of the machinery.

Vitamins and minerals

Your dog also requires a number of vitamins and minerals for good nutrition. Pet food companies typically add pre-mixes of vitamins and minerals to their food during the cooking process. However, temperatures for cooking are so high that there is a great loss of nutrition from these vitamins and minerals, so foods may be uneven.

According to the textbook Nutritional Value of Food Processing, written for food chemists in the industrial processed food industry, the changes that happen during food processing either cause nutrients to be lost or destroyed. Heat processing is harmful to the nutrients. The more severe the thermal processing, the more the nutrient content is reduced.

There may be excessive vitamin content in some batches and little in others once the pre-mixes are added. This is one reason why experts advise consumers not to count on supplements advertised in dog food, such as supplements for joint care for your dog. Another reason comes from the fact that you would have to feed your dog so much of the food to give him an adequate dose of the supplement that he would quickly become obese. If your dog requires a supplement of some kind, it is best to add it in addition to the dog food, regardless of what supplementation the food advertises. It is usually best to add vitamins and minerals to your dog's cooked meals after you have finished heating the meals. Most people mix the vitamins and minerals in with the food so their dog will not eat around them, but it can depend on the form of the vitamins and minerals. Powdered vitamins and minerals are sometimes easier to mix in with the food than capsules, for example.

The Dog's "Natural" Diet

As wolves, and for many thousands of years of early domestication, the dog's natural diet was composed of the animals it hunted. The food provided by humans only came later. This meant that the dog had to rely on the meat, the stomach contents, the intestines, organs such as the heart and liver, and the other parts of the animals it could catch. And, of course, they ate bones. The animals could vary from one part of the world to another, but they were usually mammals. Hunting in packs, wolves and dogs could also bring down larger prey. In the wild, it is not unusual for wolves to eat one large meal, such as a deer, gorge themselves, and then rest for several days while the food digests. If they cannot eat the entire animal, they may cover it up, or partially bury it, and return to it to eat more over several days. They may guard the kill, keep other predators away from it, and allow the meat on the carcass to become a little rank and smelly, which appeals to the less developed taste senses of wolves and dogs.

This is their original diet. The diet of dogs began to change as they became more domesticated and evolved from wolves to dogs as we would know them today. They became more dependent on humans for food and hunted less for themselves. This tradeoff involved a change in diet. As humans changed from hunters and gathers to farmers and developed agriculture, the canine diet changed, too. Humans stayed in one place and developed settlements and farms and towns. Dogs stayed with them to guard flocks, to offer protection, and to fulfill all of the other functions we have come to depend on dogs to do for us. No doubt dogs still received meat when it was available, but grains and cereals, milk and dairy products, perhaps even vegetables started forming part of their diet.

For the last several thousand years, wherever humans have gone, dogs have gone with us. And they have partaken of the same kind of diet we have eaten. As our own food has become more processed, so, too, has the dog's diet.

Diet and Your Dog's Health

Diet influences the overall health of dogs and affects everything from their coat and teeth to their energy levels to their weight. You have heard the saying, "You are what you eat." That is true for your dog, as well as for you. If the food you are feeding your dog is deficient in some way, you can expect to see that fact reflected in your dog's appearance and condition.

One of the best ways to know if you are feeding your dog properly is by watching his condition. Does he have good skin and coat? The skin is the

body's largest organ. If your dog has any kind of vitamin deficiency or other problem with nutrients, it often shows up first in his skin. He may have dry, itchy, or flaky skin. His hair may look dull, or he may begin to lose some of his coat. He may develop ear infections or have problems with mites and other parasites. If your dog's diet is poor, he may also have a weakened immune system, and that can cause other health problems. Some people believe that dogs with weakened immune systems are more likely to have problems with fleas, worms, and other parasites.

Are your dog's eyes bright? Is he a good weight? Is his poop small and firm? If your dog is producing waste that is large and sloppy, it is a sign that your dog's food is not agreeing with him and he is not getting much nutrition from it. If he is eating a commercial dog food, it may contain a lot of corn or wheat that your dog is having problems digesting. If your dog is gassy all the time then, again, your dog is probably having gastrointestinal problems and the food is not agreeing with him. If this is happening with your dog, change dog foods to a better quality food or consider switching to a home-cooked diet so you can manage the ingredients in your dog's diet.

The raw diet

Raw food advocates will often tell you that their dogs have pearly white teeth from eating raw meaty bones (RMBs) and living on a raw diet, but dogs that eat a homecooked diet enjoy many of the same health benefits.

Cooking your dog's meals also avoids concerns about bacteria. There are expert and veterinary concerns about feeding dogs a raw diet, especially if the dog has a compromised immune system. Dogs are able to eat raw foods and they are not as prone to problems with food bacteria as humans, but a raw diet does place a dog at greater risk from bacteria than a cooked diet.

E. coli, salmonella, and other harmful microorganisms can be health risks when feeding a raw diet. Cooking the food you feed your dog removes this concern to a great degree. The food you feed your dog on a cooked diet is no more likely to give your dog food poisoning than the food you cook for yourself.

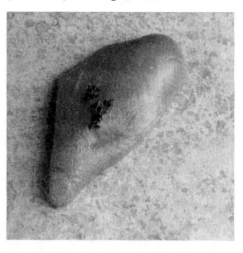

A cooked diet also avoids using fresh bones, which some people dislike feeding to their dogs for safety reasons. Impaction or obstruction in the dog's gastrointestinal tract are also concerns associated with feeding a raw diet. Eating raw, uncooked bones, while generally good for a dog's teeth, can lead to blockages in the intestines. Dogs can choke on bones if they are not ground up. Bones that are eaten or swallowed can break off into shards and puncture the stomach or intestines. There are dangers in giving a dog a bone, even if dogs and wolves have been eating bones for millennia. These dangers are greatly diminished in the cooked diet. Bones are either avoided or they are cooked with the food, which makes the bones soft and pliable, so they are not a danger.

Fresh meat protein, fresh vegetables, dairy, eggs, and the other ingredients that go into the homecooked diet can keep dogs looking and feeling good, with white teeth and clean ears without many of the concerns and risks of feeding a raw diet. Dogs that enjoy homecooked meals often live longer than is typical for dogs in their breeds and may avoid some common health problems. Canine food expert Mary Strauss, writing for the Whole Dog Journal about cooked diets writes:

"Feeding a cooked diet takes time and may cost more than feeding packaged foods (though it's possible to keep costs down by shopping sales and ethnic markets, and buying food in bulk), but the rewards are many. Dogs fed properly prepared homemade meals are usually healthier than dogs on commercial kibbled or canned diets, and you may find your vet bills are reduced. There is much joy in watching our dogs eat fresh, healthy meals we have prepared ourselves, knowing the quality of the ingredients and the value they provide, as well as the obvious enjoyment our dogs get from their food."

Along with a healthy diet, your dog also needs regular exercise in order to stay healthy. There are some exceptions for small Toy breeds but, in general, dogs need plenty of daily exercise. Regular exercise will keep your dog's muscles toned and help him stay fit, even after he reaches his senior years. A good homecooked diet can give your dog the energy to keep enjoying his exercise well into old age and may help him avoid some joint and bone problems.

The Raw Diet versus The Cooked Protein Diet

The natural diet today is usually referred to as the "raw" diet, or the BARF diet, BARF standing for Bones and Raw Food or Biologically Appropriate Raw Food. There are some differences in the raw diet, depending on which expert you read or consult.

Ian Billinghurst's diet

Dr. Ian Billinghurst is usually credited with being the first contemporary canine expert to promote a raw diet for pets. His diet emphasizes bones, meat, offal (including liver, kidneys, heart, and tripe, or the lining of a cow or other ruminant's stomach), raw vegetables such as broccoli, celery, spinach, carrots, and cayenne pepper. This selection of ingredients is considered most nutritious on the raw diet and will help your dog obtain the proper variety of vitamins and minerals. Fruits are also part of the BARF diet formulated by Dr. Billinghurst, along with whole eggs, flax seed, garlic, kelp, alfalfa, and some ingredients as supplements such as vitamin E, cod liver oil, zinc oxide, and manganese oxide. Dr. Billinghurst is completely opposed to using grains.

Dr. Billinghurst and other advocates for the raw diet feel that this kind of diet is the one that is closest to the dog's natural diet and thus healthiest for dogs. Meat, vegetables, and other ingredients do lose nutrients through the heat used in cooking, so they are more available for your dog to digest in their raw form. This is true for the meat your dog eats, although dogs can usually digest vegetables better if they are slightly cooked or puréed. You can find more information about the BARF diet on the BARFWorld website **www.barfworld.com** or by reading one of Dr. Billinghurst's books. His classic book is *Give Your Dog A Bone*.

Richard Pitcairn's diet

Another important proponent of the raw diet is Dr. Richard Pitcairn. In his book *Dr. Pitcairn's Complete Guide To Natural Health For Dogs And Cats*, he recommends a diet for dogs that includes meat, whole grains, and fresh vegetables.

Here Dr. Pitcairn differs with dog owners and breeders who try to avoid feeding their dogs much grain, though whole grains are better than highly processed grains. Grains are carbohydrates, and they provide dogs with energy, but the dog's natural diet does not include much, if any, grain. In the last few years, as more dogs seem to be developing allergies to corn and wheat, many dog owners have started turning away from feeding their dogs grains and cereals. However, dogs have been fed grains and cereals throughout history, as long as they have been domesticated, so Dr. Pitcairn has included them in his diet. Many people feed Dr. Pitcairn's diet and simply make adjustments to the amount of grains called for in the recipes or do not add them.

He also recommends supplements such as brewer's yeast, vegetable oil, cod liver oil, kelp, bone meal, vitamin E, and zinc. Dr. Pitcairn encourages people to use a variety of recipes in order to achieve a good balance of nutri-

tion. He recommends following recipes closely because they have been formulated to meet the dietary needs of your dog. He emphasizes that it is important to include calcium supplements where indicated. He suggests using organic and minimally processed foods when possible. And he says that it is important to go slowly when you are making the change in your dog's diet from commercial food to homemade or raw.

Some of the recipes he provides are for raw meals and some are for home-cooked meals, though he suggests feeding raw meats to your dog when possible. Grains and legumes need to be cooked in order for your dog to digest them properly. Some vegetables can be fed raw and others need to be cooked in Dr. Pitcairn's recipes for the same reason. In general, softer vegetables and leafy vegetables can be fed raw, but harder vegetables need to be cooked or puréed in order for your dog to be able to digest them.

Dr. Pitcairn believes this diet is closest to the natural diet of the dog without bringing in harmful chemicals that could be dangerous for your dog's health. He believes less processed food is best. Your dog will simply be healthier if you feed this diet, according to Dr. Pitcairn. Of course, Dr. Billinghurst believes the same thing about his diet and thinks you should give your dog bones.

Dr. Pitcairn also offers some vegetarian diets for dogs, though most veterinarians and canine nutritionists claim dogs cannot lead a healthy existence on a vegetarian diet.

Cooked protein

The cooked protein, or homemade, diet for dogs is not too different from these diets, at least in its ingredients. Plan on including meat, liver, and organ meat in your dog's meals, as well as eggs and dairy products. Steamed or puréed vegetables are usually included, along with some grains, legumes, or a starch. You can also add some fruit. You do not have to include all of these ingredients in each meal. It will help to plan ahead so you can balance these ingredients out over the course of a week or ten days. The proportions of what you should feed your dog should be:

Liver/kidney	5 to 10 percent
Heart	10 percent
Muscle meat and fish	the bulk of your dog's diet
Eggs	as many as your dog likes
Dairy products* (yogurt, cottage cheese)	
Vegetables	
Grains, legumes, starch	less than 25 percent
Fruit	

Yogurt and cottage cheese are usually fine, but milk can be problematic for some dogs. Some dogs are lactose intolerant, and they might have problems digesting milk. If your dog has problems digesting yogurt or cottage cheese, you can give him an antacid such as Tums to help provide calcium. Yogurt is also a probiotic containing good bacteria to help your dog's digestion. If your dog cannot eat yogurt, you will need to provide another probiotic.

Supplements will be discussed in the section on supplements, vitamins, minerals, and enzymes below.

So, the ingredients for the raw and cooked protein diets are not so different, especially not between Dr. Pitcairn's diet and the cooked diet. But most cooked diets put less emphasis on grains than Dr. Pitcairn does. They can be added to the homecooked diet, but they are not a focus of it. Many dog owners are trying to feed their dogs fewer carbohydrates because they are not believed to be a part of the dog's natural diet. Dog food companies often use lots of grains in their foods because grains can be added to the protein percentages, but meat protein is better for dogs. Your dog does not need a lot of grain or carbohydrates, from a nutritional viewpoint. Like the raw food diets, the homecooked diet does emphasize that giving your dog food made from fresh, healthy ingredients is a good way to improve your dog's health.

Going to the Vet

Prior to making any major changes in your dog's diet, it is a good idea for your dog to have a check-up from your veterinarian. Not all vets will be supportive of a plan to switch from feeding a commercial dog food to cooking at home for your dog. Most veterinarians receive standard training about nutrition in school. They might not have time to keep up or might not be open to some newer ideas about canine nutrition. They also might see dogs from some clients who have been fed on a raw or homecooked diet and have not received adequate nutrition, if the owners did not feed a nutritionally healthy diet.

You can ask your vet for advice about your dog's ideal weight and condition. Your vet should have some weight charts in his or her office to give you an idea of what a healthy dog should look like.

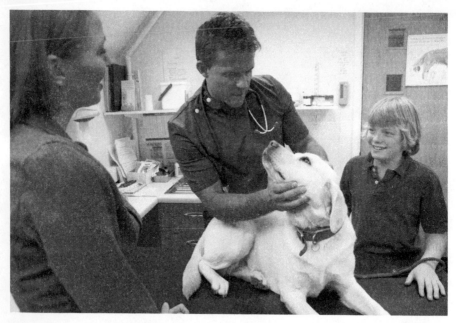

Before making a change in your dog's diet to a homecooked diet, you need to make sure your dog is in good health. If your dog has any health problems, you need to know about them before you make the change in his diet so you can plan appropriate meals. In some cases, your vet may be able to make recommendations to the diet you are planning so your dog will receive the best possible nutrition.

If your dog has certain health problems, then he may be able to particularly benefit from eating homecooked meals. For instance, dogs with allergies, irritable bowel disease, pancreatitis, kidney disease, and diabetes all often need special diets. It is often hard to find commercial dog foods that help dogs with these conditions, and owners might need to cook at home for their dogs. If your dog does have one of these conditions, or others, talk to your vet and see what kind of diet your dog needs.

CASE STUDY:
JUST WHAT THE
DOCTOR ORDERED

Anna Harlow

Anne Harlow has been homecooking for her four dogs for the last six years.

She follows a diet given to her by her holistic vet that consists of fresh meat: chicken, beef, lamb, veal, pork; fresh veggies: kale, chard, squash, carrots, potatoes, sweet potatoes, beans, peas, zucchini, and mixed greens; fresh fruits: banana, pears, peaches, blueberries, cranberries, apples without cores, and mango; and grains and pasta: rice, brown mostly, and any type of pasta noodle. "My holistic vet suggested I try it for the overall health of my dogs when they were puppies," Anne said.

None of her dogs have any special dietary requirements to work around, although her dog Hamish is sensitive to chicken and doesn't eat it as often as the other three.

"I make a "doggie stew" about twice a week in my crock pot so it doesn't take long at all," Anne said. "I use whatever I have in my fridge or have picked up at the store for the stew for the week.

"I go to Walmart on Saturday mornings when they put their weekly meat "leftovers" on 50 percent off and buy everything!"

As for recipes, Anne mostly uses the sheet provided by her holistic vet and "make things up as I go along." But she does adamantly state that her dogs much prefer her homecooked creations to any commercial food.

Anne said the biggest challenge of cooking a diet for her dogs is "making sure you provide an overall balanced diet. The diet doesn't have to be balanced on a daily basis but should be balanced overall." However, for Anne and her furry friends, the rewards far out way the challenge of home cooking. Her balanced program results in "happy, healthy dogs with shiny coats, small stool volume, and lots of energy," Anne said. Just what the doctor ordered.

And what is Anne's advice for beginners to the homecooked program?

"It's not rocket science," Anne said. "If you can cook for yourself and are healthy eating what you cook, you can certainly cook for your dogs."

Nutritional Guidelines and Tables

One of the concerns people have when they start feeding their dogs a homemade diet is that their dogs will not be getting adequate nutrition. After all, no matter what you might think of commercial dog food, you can still look on the label and find an AAFCO certification stating that the food meets minimum nutritional requirements. That is not an option when you are making your own food. It is up to you to make sure your dog's meals meet his nutritional needs.

If you feed your dog homecooked food made from healthful ingredients in the right proportions, your dog is likely to eat a nutritionally balanced diet. Just as you might not eat every vitamin and mineral required for good health in each meal you consume, your dog may not get all of his nutritional requirements in each meal. But, if you feed your dog a variety of meats and vegetables over the course of several days and weeks, then chances are good that your dog will be getting all of the nutrients he needs. Some people like to hedge their bets and add supplements to their dog's diet. There is nothing wrong with this as long as you do not over-supplement your dog.

Because you are feeding him a diet that is high in meat protein, and probably without bones, you will also need to supplement your dog's calcium so he has the proper calcium to phosphorus balance. If you are feeding meat and bones together, in a raw diet, for example, you will not need to add a calcium supplement. Meats are high in phosphorus, but in the wild, dogs usually maintain the proper calcium to phosphorus ratio because of the bones they eat. You can remedy this domesticated deficiency by adding a calcium supplement to his diet at the rate of 900 mg of calcium for each pound of food. Some people prefer to use dried and ground eggshells for their dog's calcium. You can give ½ teaspoon of dried eggshell per pound of food you feed your dog. You can even use an antacid made from calcium carbonate for this purpose.

The United States government has drawn up nutritional guidelines for dogs. These are the same guidelines followed by commercial dog food companies. They provide recommendations for how much protein and fat your dog should have, daily vitamin intake, and how many calories your dog should eat every day. These tables are included below.

DAILY RECOMMENDED ALLOWANCES FOR PROTEIN AND FATS

	PUPPIES (WEIGHING 12 LBS, 33 LBS AT MATURITY)	ADULT DOGS (WEIGHING 33 LBS)	PREGNANT/ NURSING DOGS (WEIGHING 33 LBS WITH SIX PUPPIES
Crude* Protein	56 g	25 g	69 g/158 g
Total Fat	21 g	14 g	29 g/67 g

*"Crude" refers to the specific method of testing the product, not the quality of the nutrient itself. Crude protein is the amount of protein in a food based simply on the approximate nitrogen measurement.

Table from the pamphlet *Nutrient Requirements of Dogs and Cats*, from the National Academies Press, 2006.

Weights are given in grams. If you have a kitchen scale then you should be able to weigh your ingredients in grams without any problem.

AVERAGE DAILY ENERGY NEEDS CALORIES PER DAY (Kilocalories per day*)

TYPE OF DOG	10 LBS	30 LBS	50 LBS	70 LBS	90 LBS
PUPPIES (10 lb puppy growing to 33 lbs at maturity)	990				
INACTIVE DOGS (dogs with little stimulus or opportunity to exercise)	296	674	989	1272	1540
ADULT ACTIVE DOGS (dogs with strong stimulus and ample opportunity to exercise, such as dogs in households with more than one dog, in the country or with a yard)	404	922	1353	1740	2100
PREGNANT DOGS (from 4 weeks after mating until delivery)	518	1274	1340	2570	3170
YOUNG ADULT ACTIVE DOGS	446	993	1451	1876	2264
OLDER ACTIVE DOGS	327	745	1093	1407	1700

*1 Calorie = 1 kilocalorie = 1,000 calories. The term Calorie that is used on food nutrition labels is really a "food calorie," sometimes called a "large calorie." It is equivalent to 1,000 calories (or 1 kilocalorie) as calories are defined scientifically (the amount of energy needed to warm 1 gram of water at 1 degree C). In *Nutrient Requirements of Dogs and Cats*, energy needs are expressed in terms of kilocalories, which are equivalent to Calories in this document.

Table from the pamphlet *Nutrient Requirements of Dogs and Cats*, from the National Academies Press, 2006.

The calories given here are suggestions for dogs of various weights and activity levels. Your dog might have different needs. These calorie suggestions should only be used as a starting point. You can reduce or increase calories for your dog as needed based on your dog's condition. Your dog may need more or fewer calories at different times of the year, for example. If you have a dog that is sexually intact, then your dog may have different caloric needs at different times in her estrus cycle. Always pay attention to your dog's weight and condition, and use your best judgment about how much to feed.

VITAMINS NEEDED BY DOGS

VITAMIN	WHAT IT DOES	DAILY NEEDS	DEFICIENCY RESULTS IN
Vitamin K	Activation of clotting factors, bone proteins, and other proteins	0.41 mg	No reports of naturally occurring deficiencies in normal dogs
Vitamin B1 (Thiamin)	Energy and carbohydrate metabolism; activation of ion channels in neural tissue	0.56 mg	Failure to grow, weight loss and neurological abnormalities in puppies; damage to the nervous system and to the heart in adult dogs
Riboflavin	Enzyme functions	1.3 mg	Anorexia; weight loss; muscular weakness; flaking dermatitis; eye lesions
Vitamin B6	Glucose generation; red blood cell function; niacin synthesis; nervous system function; immune response; hormone regulation; gene activation.	0.4 mg	Anorexia and weight loss in puppies; convulsions, muscle twitching, and anemia in adult dogs Impairment of motor control and balance; muscle weakness.

Niacin	Enzyme functions	4 mg	Anorexia; weight loss; inflammation of the lips, cheeks, and throat; profuse salivation; bloody diarrhea; bloody feces; convulsions
Pantothenic Acid	Energy metabolism	4 mg	Erratic food intake; sudden prostration or coma; rapid respiratory and heart rates; convulsions; gastrointestinal symptoms; reduced antibody production
Vitamin B12	Enzyme functions	9µg	Appetite loss; lack of white blood cells; anemia; bone marrow changes
Folic Acid	Amino acid and nucleotide metabolism; mitochondrial protein synthesis.	68µg	Weight loss; decline in hemoglobin concentration
Choline	Phospholipid cell membrane component	425 mg	Loss of body weight; fatty liver

*Daily needs for an adult dog weighing 33 pounds, consuming 1,000 Calories per day. g = grams; mg = milligrams; µg = micrograms

Table from the pamphlet *Nutrient Requirements of Dogs and Cats*, from the National Academies Press, 2006.

DAILY RECOMMENDED ALLOWANCES FOR MINERALS

MINERALS	FUNCTIONS	DAILY RECOMMENDED ALLOWANCES*	SIGNS OF DEFICIENCIES/ EXCESS
Calcium	Formation of bones and teeth; blood coagulation nerve impulse transmission; muscle contraction; cell signaling	0.75 g	Nutritional secondary hyperparathyroidism; significant decreases in bone mineral content, which can result in major skeletal abnormalities, especially in growing puppies of large breeds
Phosphorus	Skeletal structure; DNA and RNA structure; energy metabolism; locomotion; acid-base balance	0.75 g	Reduced weight gain; poor appetite; bowing and swelling of forelimbs in puppies

Magnesium	Enzyme functions; muscle and nerve-cell membrane stability; hormone secretion and function; mineral structure of bones and teeth	150 mg	Reduction in weight gain, irritability, and convulsions in puppies; hyperextension of carpal joints and hind-leg paralysis later in life
Sodium	Acid-base balance; regulation of osmotic pressure; nerve impulse generation and transmission	100 mg	Restlessness; increased heart rate, water intake, and hemoglobin concentration; dry and tacky mucus membranes
Potassium	Acid-base balance; nerve-impulse transmission; enzymatic reactions; transport functions impulse transmission; enzymatic	1 g	Poor growth in puppies; paralysis of neck muscles and rear legs; general weakness later in life
Chlorine	Acid-base balance; transfer of extracellular fluids across cell membranes	150 mg	Reduced weight gain and weakness in puppies
Iron	Synthesis of blood components; energy metabolism	7.5 mg	Poor growth; pale mucous membranes; lethargy; weakness; diarrhea. At acute levels, dangerous oxidative reactions that lead to gastrointestinal and other tissue damage
Copper	Connective tissue formation; iron metabolism; blood cell formation melanin pigment formation; myelin formation; defense against oxidative damage	1.5 mg	Loss of hair pigmentation in puppies; anemia
Zinc	Enzyme reactions; cell replication; protein and carbohydrate metabolism; skin function; wound healing	15 mg	Poor weight gain; vomiting; skin lesions
Manganese	Enzyme functions; bone development; neurological function	1.2 mg	No studies of deficiency in dogs

| Selenium | Defense against oxidative damage; immune response | 90 µg | Anorexia; depression; breathing discomfort; coma; muscular degeneration |
| Iodine | Thyroid hormone synthesis; cell differentiation; growth and development of puppies; regulation of metabolic rate | 220 µg | Enlargement of thyroid glands; dry, sparse hair coat; weight gain; excessive tearing, salivation, and nasal discharge; dandruff |

*Daily needs for an adult dog weighing 33 pounds, consuming 1,000 Calories per day.
g = grams; mg = milligrams; µg = micrograms

Table from the pamphlet *Nutrient Requirements of Dogs and Cats*, from the National Academies Press, 2006.

DAILY RECOMMENDED ALLOWANCES FOR VITAMINS

VITAMIN	FUNCTIONS	DAILY RECOMMENDED ALLOWANCES*	SIGNS OF DEFICIENCIES/ EXCESS
Vitamin A	Vision; growth; immune function; fetal development; cellular differentiation; transmembrane protein transfer	379µg	Anorexia; body weight loss; ataxia; conjunctivitis; corneal disorders; skin lesions; respiratory ailments; increased susceptibility to infection. Imbalance in bone remodeling processes; artery and vein degeneration; dehydration; central nervous system depression; joint pain
Vitamin D	Maintenance of mineral status; phosphorus balance	3.4µg	Rickets; lethargy; loss of muscle tone; bone swelling and bending Anorexia; weakness; diarrhea; vomiting; calcification of soft tissue; excessive mineralization of long bones; dehydration; dry and brittle hair; muscle atrophy
Vitamin E	Defense against oxidative damage	8 mg	Degeneration of skeletal muscle; reproductive failure; retinal degeneration

Table from the pamphlet *Nutrient Requirements of Dogs and Cats*, from the National Academies Press, 2006.

You should familiarize yourself with the information in these nutritional tables and consult them as needed. Do not worry if you cannot memorize all of this information by heart. That would be unrealistic. As already stated, if you feed your dog the kind of homecooked diet described in this chapter, with plenty of variety, your dog will be getting the nutrients in these tables.

Supplements, Vitamins, Minerals, and Enzymes

If you feed your dog a good homecooked diet with plenty of variety in meats and vegetables, then you probably will not need to worry too much about adding a lot of supplements to your dog's meals. However, there are some things your dog needs in his diet that you should add. Supplements can be mixed in with the food you prepare just after cooking. If you are cooking enough food for several meals, you can either add all of the supplements at one time and mix them in, or you can add the supplements to each meal as you prepare it.

Multivitamin. Most veterinarians recommend adding a good multivitamin to a dog's diet if you are cooking your own meals for your dog, especially if you are not giving other supplements. This is a good and simple way to make sure your dog is getting all of the vitamins he needs, just in case he is not getting them in his food. If you dog eats the multivitamin without any trouble, you can simply add it to his meal. If your dog is not eager to eat a vitamin tablet, you can put it in something he likes to eat and feed it to him as a treat. You can give a multivitamin made for people to your dog, such as Centrum or One A Day Maximum, bought at any drugstore. You can also give your dog a multivitamin for dogs if you prefer, but there is no difference in the vitamins. You can purchase these products at pet stores and from online pet pharmacies and pet retail merchants.

Calcium. As already mentioned, because you will be feeding your dog heavy concentrations of meat and organ meat, which are high in phosphorus, you will need to supplement your dog's calcium intake to maintain the proper calcium to phosphorus balance in his body. Add 900 mg of calcium supplement (800 to 1000 mg) for every 1 pound of food you feed your dog. You can use lots of different forms of calcium to meet your dog's need for calcium, such as calcium citrate, calcium carbonate, or calcium lactate. Calcium in these forms is commonly sold in drugstores or from health food sources online. The only thing to avoid is giving your dog a source of calcium that contains vitamin D. Your dog already gets vitamin D in his diet, and he does not need an excessive amount. Do not count dairy products as part of your dog's calcium intake. The calcium supplementation should be figured separately, as the 900 mg of calcium supplement per pound of food is in addition to the dairy calcium your dog eats.

Fish oil and taurine. Many people like to add fish oil to their dog's diet. Fish oil contains taurine, which is good for heart health. This is especially important for some breeds with heart problems, but all dogs can benefit from it. Fish oil is also a good source of omega-3 fatty acids.

Vitamin E. If you give your dog fish oil, or other kinds of oils, you need to add vitamin E to your dog's diet, too. Vitamin E is also included in the nutritional guidelines, so make sure your dog is getting enough in his diet. You can give your dog about 100 I.U.s, or international units, for every 25 pounds of body weight, twice per week. If you purchase a bottle of vitamin

E, it should have the weight listed on the bottle in international units. It is all right if you want to give your dog vitamin E on a daily basis. You can give this same amount without harm.

Cod liver oil, vitamin A, and vitamin D. Some people like to give their dogs cod liver oil. Both Dr. Billinghurst and Dr. Pitcairn include it in their diets. It contains vitamin A and D. It you are feeding your dog lots of liver, you probably do not need to give your dog cod liver oil, however, and it is possible for dogs to get too much vitamin A. If you are giving your dog cod liver oil, give them enough so that your dog is getting about 100 I.U.s of vitamin D for every 20 pounds of body weight per day.

Green blends and seaweed. Many people like to give their dogs a green blend or a seaweed mix that contains kelp and alfalfa to make sure their dogs are getting enough iodine in their diet. Iodine is important to maintain the proper function of the thyroid gland. All animals need trace minerals in their diet. Although dogs and other animals only need minute amounts of these minerals, they perform important functions in the body. Iron regulates hemoglobin in the dog's red blood cells and is vital for a dog's health. Other trace minerals for dogs include zinc, manganese, copper, iodine, and selenium. Make sure your dog is getting enough trace minerals in some form.

Other supplements that people sometimes include in their dogs' diets include garlic, honey, apple cider vinegar, brewer's yeast, and molasses. Some people have their own favorites and personal formulas. Supplements such as these can add specific vitamins or are said to be good for different functions.

Remember that the only supplement you really must add to your home-cooked diet is the calcium supplement and a good multivitamin, if you are inclined. Other supplements are optional.

It is not generally necessary to include things such as prebiotic or probiotic enzymes in your dog's cooked diet because these are included as part of the diet in the form of dairy (yogurt) and the other foods you are preparing. Probiotics are the "good bacteria" that your dog eats to keep his gut in good working order. When good bacteria flourish, they keep bad bacteria away. Bad bacteria can lead to diarrhea, vomiting, and other stomach problems. The good bacteria help your dog digest his food properly and keep your dog's gastrointestinal system in good working order. The most popular and easy-to-use probiotic is yogurt, but there are others. You can buy probiotics that are made especially for the purpose of helping with your dog's digestion. You are buying bacteria, but it comes in a form that is easy to give to your dog. You can purchase Baccillus coagulans at Amazon.com; Enterococcus faecium in different supplements for your dog such as Fortiflora made by Purina; and Bifiobacterium animalis, which comes in a product called Probiotic Miracle.

Prebiotics are similar to probiotics. They also nourish your dog's gastrointestinal system, but they provide nourishment for the good bacteria that benefits your dog's system. Some prebiotics include inulin, larch, and chicory. You can often find both probiotics and prebiotics for sale at pet stores and from online pet product retailers. You can also find them at health stores.

Keep in mind that cooking will destroy some of the vitamins in your dog's food, and so will freezing it. Preparing food for your dog at home may be healthier than feeding him a commercial diet, but food is healthiest when it is freshest. The longer things cook, the more the vitamins and other good things in the food break down. The same goes with freezing the food.

CASE STUDY: MULTIPLE DOGS WITH DIFFERENT FOOD ALLERGIES
Pat Boldt

Pat Boldt has been homecooking for her dogs for more than 15 years. She currently has ten dogs enjoying or transitioning to her homecooking.

I feed a partial homecooked, partially raw, partial commercial diet. With multiple dogs, each has a specific need, and juggling each dog's needs with the best food and preparing for ten different dogs daily is difficult. A routine is required. I use coat quality and texture and stools when determining what is working best for each.

I started feeding a homecooked diet because of my dogs' food intolerances and food allergies. We did a VARL blood serum test on all three dogs with food allergies. Jamie, a Gordon Setter, is allergic to beef, oats, and rice. Patrick, an Irish Setter, is allergic to lamb, oats, and eggs. Sydney, another Irish Setter, is allergic to eggs and potatoes. Therefore, they each have their individualized diets, and most are on modified diets. Patrick's diet is closest to a homemade and raw-only diet. Although I've read several different diet books and have used one book in the past in particular, I modify each diet to each dog's specific needs. There is *no* one size fits all.

I also decided to homecook after a bad experience with commercial feed. I used one "premium" dog kibble that turned the dogs' coats all orange after six months of use. And this was a very expensive brand! It took a year to get their coats back to normal.

As for recipes, I started with Monica Segal's homemade diet book. It's the best on the market, and I have referred it to everyone. She has several now. Then I modified them to make them work for me. It was all trial and error. Once you figure it out — although you may tear your hair out trying to do elimination diets, which is adding one thing in at a time and writing things down — it's easy. You just stick to what works.

Because of all the food allergies, eat dog gets a specific set of ingredients. I have raw-primal duck for Patrick, and cooked, boiled, or barbecue chicken for everyone except the puppies. I give out Natural Balance limited ingredients kibble — potato and duck for all adults except Sydney, who is allergic to potatoes, and lamb and rice for the puppies, who are now 1 year old. They will be transitioned to homecooked meals at 18 months. I also give out canned Evangers Kosher chicken to everyone, buffalo to Patrick, and lamb and rice to the puppies. The supplements I add vary per dog. I add vegetables based on what is available in the season, usually carrots, broccoli, etc. I give raw beef marrow bones to all for cleaning teeth weekly.

It takes about one hour to feed ten dogs per feeding. This includes prep time, feeding, and cleanup. Cooked chicken and fresh vegetables are usually prepared in bulk twice a week. I use boiled chicken 80 percent of the time, but sometimes I add barbecued skinless chicken breasts for a change. However, two of the dogs get a looser stool just from that little bit more grease, so boiled is always preferred and can be easily cooked and frozen.

I watch for chicken on sale at stores, usually chicken breasts with rib meat at 99 cents per pound, boneless skinless breasts at $1.97 or 1.99 per pound, and whole chickens for oven cooking in the wintertime for 89 cents per pound, sometimes lower. These are California prices.

I sometimes use organic chicken if it is on sale. I usually get my fruits and vegetables from a farmers market. Farmers markets are always better than the store and are readily available here in California.

I get carrots and other veggies at Sam's club or a farmers market organic grower.

I buy canned foods by the case, and I belong to several Breeder programs. For example, Natural Balance has a buy-ten-bags-get-one-free deal. Evangers canned food is buy five cases and get one free. My pet food store does all paperwork for Natural Balance, but with Evangers, you need to send in your receipts. But both programs are very easy and very worthwhile. I save between $400.00 to $500.00 per year because of these programs.

I would recommend homecooking to others, but you need to be dedicated and find your routine to make it work. I can make it work for ten dogs pretty easily.

If you have multiple dogs and have to have multiple homecooked diets, find the commonality between them. What vegetables and protein source do they have in common? Make it as simple as possible.

The biggest challenge to homecooking is finding your routine to make it work without driving yourself crazy. Well, that and finding enough counter space for ten dogs! And the biggest reward of homecooking is of course happy, healthy dogs!

Foods Your Dog Should Not Eat

There are a number of foods you should not feed your dog for various reasons. You may have seen similar lists online, and they are usually accurate. Here are some foods to make sure your dog avoids:

- Alcohol
- Avocado pits, and other pitted foods
- Caffeine
- Chocolate
- Grapes and raisins
- Macadamia nuts
- Mushrooms
- Nutmeg
- Onions, and garlic in large amounts
- Sugar
- Xylitol (found in sugarless chewing gum, human toothpaste, and some other products)

You will sometimes find onions and garlic included as ingredients in dog food or dog food recipes. Some people give garlic as a daily supplement. Small amounts of these ingredients probably will not harm your dog. However, if your dog eats them in large amounts, they can be dangerous. Onions have been linked to hemolytic anemia, which can be fatal to dogs. It is best not to give your dog onion at all. You can safely give your dog about half of a small clove of garlic for every 20 pounds of body weight.

These are the most serious things you should keep away from your dog. Use common sense and do not give your dog things to eat such as salt, moldy food, or garbage. Your dog is not a garbage disposal; do not give him things to eat that should be tossed out. Leftovers are fine, but do not give your dog something you would not eat yourself.

The next chapter will look at some of the things you should consider and do before you change your dog to a homecooked diet.

Chapter 4

Before You Start

he last chapter looked at the dog's natural diet and how it became modified over time to be similar to the diet humans eat. The chapter also looked at commercial dog food diets and compared raw diets with cooked protein diets. It provided nutritional guidelines and information to help you create a healthy home-cooked diet for your dog.

This chapter will consider the practical things to do before you start cooking for your dog. Changing your dog's diet from eating a commercial food for every meal to eating a more natural, homecooked diet can be drastic. You may want to get advice from an expert before making this change, and several options for getting a second opinion are discussed. You will likely need to get some appliances and things for your kitchen so you have everything you need to get started cooking for your dog. There are some tips on shopping and buying ingredients that can save you money. There are also some tips on preparation and cooking that can save you time in the kitchen. Then there is the subject of organic versus nonorganic ingredients. Finally, the chapter will present a timeline for changing your dog over to a cooked diet in order to minimize any gastrointestinal problems.

Veterinarians and Canine Nutritionists

As mentioned in the last chapter, before you switch your dog over to eating a homecooked diet, it is a good idea to have your dog checked out by your veterinarian to make sure he is healthy and that he does not have any underlying health issues that need special attention. If he does have a health problem, you need to know about it so you can tailor his diet to address it and develop the right diet for the problem. Special health conditions that might need special diets include diabetes, allergies, kidney problems, liver disease, bladder stones, and heart disease. You will find recipes for some of these health issues in this book.

Your veterinarian might not be completely supportive of your intention to put your dog on a homecooked diet. Depending on your vet's age, when he or she went to school, how much he or she has kept up with nutritional changes, and other factors, your vet may try to discourage you from putting your dog on a homecooked diet. It is also possible that your vet has had some bad experiences with dogs that were fed a raw or homecooked diet and the owners did not do a good job with the diet. Do talk to your vet about feeding your dog a homecooked diet and listen to what he or she has to say. However, do not be discouraged if he or she is not encouraging.

If you would like the opinion of an expert in canine nutrition about your dog's diet, then you can consult with a canine nutritionist. You might not have one in your area, but you can find them online. Lew Olson at **www.b-naturals.com/newsletter** is a well-known and widely-published canine food expert with a Ph.D. in Natural Nutrition who is often consulted, and so is canine nutritionist Monica Segal, AHCW, author of *K9 Kitchen, Your Dog's Diet: The Truth Behind the Hype,* and *Optimal Nutrition: Raw and Cooked Canine Diets.* You can find others online. Nutritionists do charge for consultations, but they often have newsletters, email lists, and books that provide good information. Canine nutritionists keep up with the latest information and nutritional studies about dogs and what they need in their diets. They are usually the best sources of information about what you should be feeding your dog. If you have a consultation with a canine nutritionist, he or she can look at the diet you are feeding your dog, evaluate your ingredients, look at the calories your dog is getting, as well as your dog's age, weight, breed, and other considerations, and make suggestions to improve the diet. They can make sure your dog's diet is not deficient in any nutrients and recommend any supplements you dog might need. If you are having any problems with your dog's diet, these are the experts to go to.

Do not be discouraged if the nutritional information you read changes. A diet that was considered the healthiest possible diet for your dog five years ago may be slightly out of date now, and the ingredients might need to be adjusted or the percentages might need to be tweaked. This is because there is a great deal of ongoing research about dog nutrition, and researchers are learning new things all the time to make dogs healthier. In just the last several years, there has been a much greater emphasis on protein in canine diets, and no-grain diets have become popular. The diets described by Dr. Pitcairn, which emphasize whole grains, are not in favor as much as they once were.

This is partly due to the allergies that some dogs have experienced that have been attributed to wheat and corn. Some owners believe that grains can lead to other illnesses in dogs. The research does not necessarily support these beliefs, but dog food companies are making more foods that are

grain-free to attract customers who believe these things. People feeding raw diets and home-made diets generally cut down or cut out grain in their dogs' meals now. The number of dogs that have allergies is still small compared to the entire dog population. Food allergies account for about 10 percent of allergies, according to veterinarians.

Among dogs that do have food allergies, grains are not at the top of the list. More dogs are allergic to meat proteins than are allergic to grains. It is hard to say if this emphasis on no-grain diets will continue. It will depend on what future research reveals and what dog owners believe. *In chapter 6 of this book, you will find some recipes for dogs with allergies and dogs that need to eat gluten-free meals.* There are also some recipes for dogs that cannot eat common proteins such as chicken or beef and that require novel proteins, such as bison, venison, and duck, instead.

For Your Kitchen

Before your start making any food for your dog, you will need to have some things in your kitchen to make the process easier. If you are one of those fortunate people who has a well-stocked and well-appointed kitchen, with wonderful appliances and gadgets, you might already have everything you need to start making your dog's food. But, for the rest of us, it might be necessary to go buy a few things.

Here are some things that can make cooking for your dog easier:

- Food processor
- Meat grinder
- Resealable containers (Tupperware type)
- Big spoons
- Mixing bowls
- Rolling pin (for making cookies and treats)
- Pans for baking (loaf pans, cupcake pan, muffin pans, cake pans)
- Assorted pots and pans
- Baggies or Glad Lock® bags
- Measuring cup
- Measuring spoons
- Cutting board
- Kitchen scale (grams and ounces)

You will probably find a few other things you need as you encounter various recipes, but these are the main kitchen appliances you will need.

One item you might want to invest in is a small freezer, especially if you intend to buy bulk amounts of meat to save money. A small freezer chest may cost you several hundred dollars, so you might want to wait until you see if you intend to continue homecooking for your dog before making this kind of investment. A small freezer chest from Walmart is $229.

You might be worried about using the same appliances you use to make your family's food for your dog, but this is not something that should concern you. You will be using the same cuts of meat, the same vegetables, and other ingredients that you would use for your own food to make your dog's food. There is no difference in the ingredients. You could eat your dog's food, if you wished. There will not be anything in the food that is second-rate or that should make you hesitate to handle it or eat it. Some of the recipes here are simply modified versions of human meals. Use the same hygienic food handling practices with your dog's food that you use for your own food.

When it comes to storing your dog's food in the refrigerator or freezer, you should label it. It will presumably be in a resealable container or in a plastic bag for freezing. Simply write on a label that it is Sparky's food, the date, and what it is. There should not be any reason to mix your dog's food up with your spouse's lunch. Or, your spouse might find that he or she enjoys Sparky's food. The food will be perfectly edible and nutritious, if a little heavy on the liver.

As mentioned previously, if you decide you will continue to homecook for your dog on a long-term basis, you might want to buy a small chest freezer so you can buy meats in bulk. You can save money buying meat this way.

Shopping and buying ingredients

There are different ways you can go about shopping for your dog if you are homecooking. If you have one small dog, you can simply include your dog's shopping when you are buying your own food. You can buy family packs of chicken or hamburger, and it will make enough food for your dog for several days. You can also buy family packs of pork or lamb and do the same thing. You can buy your vegetables and fruit from the produce aisle when you are buying yours. Or, you could visit a local farmers market if you prefer. The point is, if you have one small dog, homecooking is simple. It can be an extension of cooking for yourself.

If you have a larger dog, or if you have several dogs, homecooking begins to demand more preparation and planning. Cost starts to become an issue. In order to save money and keep homecooking affordable, it is a good idea

to check around to see if you have some friends who also cook for their dogs or who feed their dogs a raw diet. If you have dog friends, you might know someone who does cook for his or her dogs or feeds raw. In that case, you can get together to place a bulk order for various kinds of meat. This works well if you have a small freezer chest and you can store the meat. If you live in a rural area, you can visit a local farmers co-op and ask for farmers who sell half or quarter sides of beef, pork, or lamb. You and your friends can have the meat cut up any way you like. Farmers might also be willing to keep you supplied with fresh vegetables, in season. Check sites such as SustainableEats.com for more information about buying bulk meat at **www.sustainableeats. com/2010/02/18/buying-bulk-meat-what-you-need-to-know**.

If you live in an urban area, it might cost you a little more to get large quantities of beef, pork, or lamb, but you can order them from butchers. Some farmers will sell directly to consumers online, so you can still buy directly from the farm if that is important to you.

Remember to check farmers markets in your area, in season, and visit farms that allow you to go in the fields and pick your own produce and fruits. And do not forget that you can grow your own vegetables and fruits. Doing a little farming yourself is a great way to have fresh veggies and fruits for your dog's meals. You can easily grow some broccoli, carrots, squash, and other vegetables that dogs love in your own garden.

Organic or nonorganic?

Many people like the idea of feeding their dogs organic foods: organic meats, organic vegetables, organic fruits, and so on. However, according to the FDA and the USDA, organic foods are not necessarily healthier or safer for consumers. That might seem counterintuitive, but there are some reasons to justify that position. For example, animals raised organically are not wormed with the same chemical wormers that conventionally raised animals receive. There are no natural wormers that approach the effectiveness of chemical wormers. As a result, organically raised animals carry a much higher parasite load than other animals. Unless they become ill, at which time they are usually treated with chemicals and they are no longer considered organic, these animals do have worms and other parasites at the time they are butchered. The same is true for the way they are raised in general. They do not receive treatment or vaccinations for most illnesses, unless they become sick, when they are taken out of the organic herd. So, these animals are the ones that are being processed and sold as organic meat. "Organic" sounds good, but it does not always mean the animals are the healthiest animals.

On the other hand, animals that are raised conventionally do receive lots of chemicals. They are treated for worms, they are vaccinated, and they are treated with chemicals if they become sick. They usually appear to be quite healthy, but if you feed your dog meat from these animals, you might be passing along chemicals they received.

Organic meat usually costs much more than conventionally raised meat, which is another consideration.

The same is true for vegetables and other ingredients; organic vegetables and other ingredients often cost much more than conventionally grown produce. Anything raised without chemicals is often more labor-intensive, and those costs are passed along to the consumer.

It is up to you whether you want to spend the additional money to buy organic food for your dog. There are pros and cons to organic meat and vegetables. There are many people who cook for their dogs using organic foods, and there are many others who use conventional meat and vegetables. The fact that you are cooking for your dog is ultimately more important than whether the ingredients are organic.

Kitchen efficiency

Making your dog's food is time consuming. You should know that before you begin. But that does not mean you have to spend all day in the kitchen or that you have to cook for your dog every day. With a little planning, you can prepare a week's worth of meals for your dog in one day, freeze them, and then have them ready to feed to your dog for each meal.

For example, for a dog that weighs 50 pounds, you could easily prepare the following mixture:

5.25 lbs. of hamburger

28 oz. of yogurt

14 oz. of liver

2.5 lbs. of puréed vegetables

9450 mg. of calcium

14 fish oil capsules

0.25 oz. of green blend (kelp and alfalfa)

That is enough food for 14 meals. After cooking the meat, liver, and vegetables and adding the yogurt and other ingredients, you can simply divide up the meal and seal it in resealable containers. Label the food with your dog's name, the date, and what is in the container, and your dog's meals are prepared for a week. You can wait to add the fish oil capsules and the green blend individually to each meal so the vitamins and minerals will stay fresh and potent. Simply heat up each meal as you take it out of the freezer, and your dog can enjoy your homecooking without a ton of time in the kitchen.

This kind of cooking does not require you to spend a long time, but it does mean you will need to plan your meals in advance so you know what to buy at the store. Your refrigerator will be full of things such as liver and yogurt waiting to be used, and you will always have vegetables in your vegetable bin.

It is a good idea to label some of these ingredients so your spouse or children do not grab them by accident. This is not because the food would be bad for your family, but because you should make sure the ingredients are undisturbed by someone reaching in the refrigerator and grabbing your dog's cottage cheese. You can also set aside a shelf in your kitchen cabinet for things such as your green blend, your calcium supplement, and other things you often add to your dog's meals. It will help you be more efficient in the kitchen if you are organized and keep things in a specific place.

One thing you will probably want to keep on hand is a stash of canned fish, such as mackerel, sardines, or salmon. It is fine to substitute canned fish for meat in some of your dog's meals. Plus, there may be times when you have forgotten or not had time to make anything for your dog's dinner. It is easy to pull out a can of fish and add a few vegetables to it for your dog's supper. Most dogs are crazy about canned fish. You will obviously not want to give your dog fish for every meal. Fish, hamburger, chicken, pork, and so on, all have different amino acids. Your dog needs all of them. That is why you should cook your dog a variety of meats and vegetables. He will be able to get the nutrients he needs on a rotating basis. When you do give your dog canned fish such as these, there is no need to add extra calcium to the meal because these fish have small bones in them. They will not hurt your dog, so there is no need to worry. Watch your grocery store for times when they have sales on canned fish, and you can stock up. In fact, watch your store for when they have sales on anything. You never know when they might have sales that could provide you with things you might need for your dog's meals. Browse through some of the recipes in this book to get an idea of some of the ingredients you might need in the future.

CASE STUDY: STEWS AND KIBBLE

CLASSIFIED CASE STUDIES

directly from the experts

Jill Baum

Jill Baum has been homecooking for her dogs for about ten years.

I switched to a homecooked diet because I wanted more control of what my dogs ate, and I wanted them to have more meat (within the constraints of a very busy lifestyle), with fresh vegetables, and no added sugar or grain.

I feed a kibble base — Kirkland chicken and rice, with lamb and rice or salmon and potato rotated in. I make a chicken and vegetable based stew (if beef or pork is on a really good sale, sometimes it is beef or pork based with vegetables). Organ meats are rotated in, and the vegetables change, although the most frequent vegetables are carrots, peas, broccoli, spinach, and green beans. I don't use actual recipes; I just made it up as I went along. The dogs like their kibble and stew very well, but when I feed raw chicken (which I do about once a week), they like that even better.

I make a large crock pot every week or ten days. The crock pot cooks on low for two days, then cools and is divided into containers and refrigerated or frozen. So I spend maybe half an hour a week on preparing and cooking food for my dogs.

I buy 10 lb. bags of chicken leg quarters and rotate in other ingredients, such as ground beef, pork shoulder, and chicken livers and/or gizzards. I only use organic food if it is on sale.

Since switching to a homecooked diet, my dogs' health has been excellent. They all have good teeth and weight and shiny coats. The biggest reward of homecooking for me is knowing that my dogs are getting more meat and less sugar and grain.

I recommend homecooking to others frequently. My advice is to decide how much time you have, and how much you want to do, then do your research. If you are doing 100 percent homecooked, make sure you have a balanced diet. Also, make sure you have the storage room for raw or cooked ingredients.

Switching to the New Diet

Nutritionists recommend giving your dog about three weeks when making the change over to the new, homecooked diet. You will need to go slowly because your dog is used to eating a commercial diet. You will especially need to go slowly if your dog has always eaten dry kibble. Dogs have a reputation for being able to eat anything, but some dogs have a sensitive gastrointestinal tract. Your dog can easily develop diarrhea or other stomach problems when making the switch.

You can start by mixing some yogurt in with your dog's regular food and slowly start adding some cooked meat and rice to his meals. Rice is easy to digest, and your dog should be able to start getting used to this kind of homecooking. You can gradually, over several days, begin adding a little more meat to your dog's diet, along with some vegetables. Be careful with the vegetables, as the fiber in them can cause some dogs to start having some issues with diarrhea. Remember to go slowly.

You could also start by giving your dog some leafy vegetables. The softer, leafy vegetables are easier for your dog to digest than vegetables that have to be puréed or softened for your dog to eat, such as broccoli, although most dogs like raw broccoli. Let your dog get used to each step, and make sure his poop is normal before adding more of the homecooked diet. By about three weeks, your dog should be eating an entirely homecooked meal and having normal bowel movements. If not, go back to the step he was last having normal bowel movements and stay there for a bit longer until he adjusts. Be sure you are adding the calcium supplement and a multivitamin to his diet so he is getting the nutrients he needs.

After your dog has made the change to the homecooked diet, it is important that you continue to assess his skin and coat, his weight, and his overall condition on a daily basis. You can keep a journal about your dog's condition if it will help you remember his progress. Write down his weight, what you are feeding him, what supplements you are giving him (if any besides calcium and a multivitamin), and how his bowel movements look. Keep track of how he is doing to make sure he is staying healthy on the new diet.

The next chapter will look at some delicious doggie meals! It is time for Basic Mealtime Recipes.

Chapter 5

Basic Mealtime Recipes

ooking for your dog is a lot like cooking for yourself or your family. In fact, you would not go far wrong if you pulled out your grandmother's cookbook and used some recipes to make stews and casseroles for your dog, omitting the onions and anything else harmful to dogs. The basic mealtime recipes presented here are all delicious, and you could eat them yourself if you chose. These recipes are for healthy adult dogs that do not have any allergies or other problems with food, and they are intended for everyday meal times. The only supplement you will consistently need to add to your dog's diet is calcium because the recipes do not include bones (unless they feature canned fish). Give your dog between 800 and 1000 mg of calcium per pound of food. You should also give your dog a multivitamin each day to make sure he is getting all of his vitamins on a regular basis. Otherwise, his needs should be met through the food he eats as long as you feed him a variety of food each week, including different meats, organs, fats, carbs, vegetables, dairy, and fruits, just as you eat for yourself.

If you are making meals that feature fish and are using canned fish, such as tuna, salmon, or jack mackerel, you can reduce the amount of calcium

you add to the food by half. Canned fish includes bones that supply your dog with some of the calcium he needs. The fish has been pressure cooked so the bones are soft, so they will not hurt your dog when he eats them.

The recipes presented here include the ingredients you need to make them, how to prepare them, the serving size, how many servings each recipe makes, and any special serving instructions. They also include some accompaniments you can add to the dishes, as well as helpful tips about nutrition and cooking.

These recipes generally make three to four pounds of food. That is enough food for more than two meals for most dogs, depending on the size of your dog. You will probably need to store some of the food unless you have more than one dog. These meals do not have any preservatives in them. They are just like your own leftovers. You can store them in your refrigerator in a resealable bag or in a Tupperware type container. If you store the food in your refrigerator, be sure to label what the food is and when it was made so you can use it before it goes bad. Most of these meals will be good in the refrigerator for several days. Or, you can freeze the leftovers and pull them out when you need them. Whether the food is in the refrigerator or coming from the freezer, be sure to warm it up appropriately before giving it to your dog to eat. He will like the food much better if it is at the right temperature for eating and is not too cold.

One thing to remember about the meals presented here is that they should be used as starting points. They have been tried and taste-tested by real dogs, and they work. But your dog may have different tastes. So, try some recipes and see how your dog likes them. Next time you make the recipe, feel free to play with it. You are the cook, so make it your own. If your dog does not care for broccoli, then get rid of it and use carrots instead. If your dog dislikes fruit, leave the fruit out of a meal. Maybe you can add a little Parmesan cheese to a meal, and your dog will love it. You know your dog better than anyone and you are cooking for him, so make the recipes the way he will like them.

Bon appétit.

Recipe #1: Chicken and Broccoli

Prep time: 20 minutes; makes ten 1-cup servings

Ingredients:

> 3 lbs. skinless chicken, whole or
>   in pieces
> 1 cup (about 6 ounces) barley
> 4 eggs
> 2 cups broccoli, puréed
> ¼ cup chopped peanuts

You can substitute other vegetables if your dog is not fond of broccoli.

Instructions:

Preheat oven to 350 degrees F. Lightly grease a roasting pan.

Roast the chicken until the juices run clear when pierced with a fork or skewer. This usually takes 20 to 30 minutes for breasts or thighs; 45 to 60 minutes for a whole chicken. Allow the chicken to cool.

Cook the barley using the package directions.

Remove the bones from the chicken and chop it into large pieces.

Lightly beat eggs and pour into a pan; add puréed broccoli. Cook together for about five minutes until the egg mixture begins to firm up. Let cool.

Stir the egg mixture with the chicken, barley, and the peanuts.

Accompaniments:

You can add some plain yogurt as a topping to this meal, or sprinkle some alfalfa sprouts on it to add a little extra green to your dog's diet. Alfalfa sprouts can help your dog get some of the trace minerals he needs in his diet.

Tips:

Peanuts are not actually nuts. They are a legume, like peas. They have a high fat content, but they are high in protein, too, as well as antioxidants and vitamin E. If your dog likes nuts, you can use pecans, walnuts, cashews, almonds, or other nuts in this recipe. But do not use macadamia nuts. They are toxic to dogs.

If your dog needs to gain weight, or if he is a working dog that uses lots of energy, you can use chicken that still has the skin for this recipe. It will add a few more calories to the dish.

Recipe #2: Pork and Beans

Prep time: Five minutes; makes ten 1-cup servings

Ingredients:

> 3 lbs. pork
> 1 cup cooked, chopped green beans
>   (or peas)
> 1 cup grated Cheddar cheese
> 2 cups brown rice

Instructions:

Cut the pork meat into large pieces and cook on the stove top over medium heat for about 20 minutes or until the meat is no longer pink and the juices from the meat run clear when tested with a fork or skewer.

Cook the brown rice according to the package directions.

Take the pork from the pan and add the Cheddar cheese. Allow it to cool.

Mix the green beans and rice into the pork mixture.

Accompaniments:

You can add some fruit to this recipe such as an apple. Apples go great with pork and Cheddar cheese.

Tips:

You can use just about any kind of pork for this recipe, with the possible exception of spicy or hot sausage. If you use pork chops or a pork cut that contains a bone, remove the bone after cooking and before you give the meat to your dog.

Some owners wonder whether it is okay to give their dog pork to eat. The answer is an emphatic Yes! Dogs have no trouble eating and digesting pork. Pork is included in some expensive dog foods, too. Simply follow sensible preparation and cooking guidelines when making pork dishes for your dog.

Recipe #3: Pasta Feast

Prep time: 15 minutes; makes eight 1-cup servings

Ingredients:

4 lbs. lean ground beef or chuck steak

1 medium tomato, diced

¼ cup Parmesan cheese, grated

8 oz. your dog's favorite pasta

8 oz. cooked, chopped green beans

Instructions:

Cook the beef in a pan on the stove top over a medium heat for about 15 minutes until the meat is brown and the meat juices run clear.

Stir in the diced tomato and the Parmesan cheese. Remove the mixture from the heat. Allow to cool.

Cook the pasta according to the package directions. Drain. Add the pasta to the meat mixture.

Add the green beans to the meat and pasta mixture. Let the mixture cool and serve.

Accompaniments:

You can top this delicious pasta dish off with some yogurt to make it complete.

Tips:

Tomatoes belong to the nightshade family and they are not recommended for dogs that have arthritis. The same goes for potatoes and eggplant. You can still make this dish without the tomato. Try adding some carrots or squash instead.

Recipe #4: Beef and Chicken

Prep time: 20 minutes; makes 12 1-cup servings

Ingredients:

   4 lbs. skinless chicken, whole or in pieces

   8 oz. beef livers

   1 cup grated carrots

2 cups barley

½ cup Cheddar cheese, grated

Instructions:

Preheat oven to 350 degrees F. Lightly grease a roasting pan.

Roast the chicken until the juices run clear when pierced with a fork or skewer. This usually takes 20 to 30 minutes for breasts or thighs; 45 to 60 minutes for a whole chicken. Allow the chicken to cool.

Remove the bones from the chicken and cut the meat into large pieces.

Simmer beef livers in a saucepan with a small amount of water for about 20 minutes until they are thoroughly cooked. Allow them to cool.

Cook the barley according to the package directions.

Cut up the livers and mix all of the ingredients together.

Accompaniments:

If your dog likes fruit, you can add a little cranberry sauce to this dish to make it even more appetizing. Cranberries are a great source of antioxidants.

Tips:

Beef and chicken are basic ingredients. You can change this recipe in many ways. You can use turkey instead of chicken, for example. Or you can use chicken livers instead of beef livers. Use a different vegetable if your dog gets tired of carrots. Use your imagination and this recipe can always stay interesting.

Recipe #5: Turkey and Gravy

Prep time: 30 minutes; makes nine 1-cup servings

Ingredients:

> 3 lbs. turkey pieces
>
> 1 cup oatmeal
>
> 1 lb. sweet potatoes, cubed
>
> 2 Tbsp. cranberry sauce
>
> 4 Tbsp. turkey gravy* (see gravy recipe below)

Instructions:

Preheat oven to 350 degrees F. Lightly grease a roasting pan.

Roast the turkey pieces until the juices run clear when pierced by a fork or skewer. This usually takes 30 to 45 minutes for a boneless breast or thigh; 45 to 60 minutes for a breast or thigh with bone; and one and a half to two hours for an entire turkey, depending on its size.

Remove all of the bones from the turkey and cut the meat into large pieces. Save the pan juices to use for making the turkey gravy.

Cook raw sweet potatoes with the turkey for 25 to 30 minutes or until soft. Allow to cool, then peel and dice.

Cook the oatmeal according to package directions.

Mix together the turkey, sweet potatoes, oatmeal, and cranberry sauce. Pour the turkey gravy over the mixture.

*Turkey Gravy instructions:

Melt a tablespoon of butter in a saucepan over medium heat.

Add a tablespoon of flour to the butter. Any kind of flour is okay. It is a thickening agent in this case.

Slowly add the pan juices from the roasted turkey pieces and stir them into the flour and butter mixture. You can strain the juices first if there are any larger pieces from the turkey in them. Slowly bring the mixture to a boil while you stir, then remove from heat. You can serve the gravy warm.

Accompaniments:

This recipe makes a wonderful Thanksgiving dinner for your dog, so you can add some tasty Thanksgiving trimmings to it. Add a little canned pumpkin for a doggy dessert, for example (not the pie filling, which is too spicy for dogs). Skip the whipped cream, but you can use some plain yogurt instead.

Tips:

Sweet potatoes are used in this recipe. They are great for dogs and they are one of the most nutritious of vegetables. Many dogs love them. You can substitute them in lots of recipes if your dog likes them. They are easy to cook: you can boil them, roast them, microwave them, mash them, bake them, and generally cook them the same way you would potatoes. Try them for your dog and see how he likes them.

Recipe #6: Potluck

Prep time: 15 minutes; makes ten 1-cup servings

Ingredients:

 3 lbs. ground pork

 3 lbs. beef heart

 1 cup quinoa

 ½ cup grated carrots

 1 medium apple, diced

Instructions:

Cook the pork in a pan over medium heat for about 15 minutes until the meat is no longer pink and the juices run clear when tested with a fork or skewer.

Cook the quinoa following package directions.

Simmer the heart in a large saucepan, with a small amount of water, for about 45 to 60 minutes until it is thoroughly cooked. When it is done the heart should still feel firm. It should not be falling apart.

Drain the water from the heart and allow it to cool. Cut into small pieces.

Mix the quinoa with the pork and the heart. Allow them to cool and set aside.

Mix the apple and carrots together. Then mix them into the pork and heart.

Accompaniments:

This recipe is quite rich, with the heart included, but you can top it off with a tablespoon of honey to give it a nice finishing touch.

Tips:

Quinoa and couscous are two grain-related products you might not have in your kitchen. They make a nice change for your dog from the usual kinds of grains he eats. Quinoa (pronounced kee-nwah) is closely related to spinach, though it is a seed. The seeds are fluffy and creamy, and they have a

nutty taste when cooked. Quinoa is also a little crunchy. Your dog should like it when he tries it. Quinoa is an ancient food and was used by the Incas. It is high in protein as well as some trace minerals such as manganese.

Quinoa cooks quickly, so you might want to add a little extra water to your pot when cooking it for your dog. This will make it slightly softer and more digestible. If you are buying quinoa from bulk bins in your grocery store you should be sure to rinse it thoroughly. Otherwise it will be bitter. Quinoa has a natural protective coating that gives it a bitter taste unless you wash it well. Quinoa is more expensive than rice and some other grains, especially if you buy it in the grocery store. It usually costs less if you buy it through a food co-op. If you will be buying a lot of quinoa, such as if your dog has allergies for example, then you should check out the prices for larger amounts on Amazon.com and at the large discount stores. You can easily buy four pounds of quinoa on Amazon.com **www.amazon.com/ Earthly-Delights-Organic-Premium-Percent/dp/B0036FB6FY/ref=sr_ 1_3?ie=UTF8&qid=1317068968&sr=8-3** for $22 or at CostCo for $10, while 12 ounces might cost $6 or more in the grocery store.

Couscous is a food staple in West Africa and it is a kind of pasta or semolina made from wheat flour. It is versatile and you can use it for breakfast meals, dinner, special occasion meals, and so on. There are countless recipes for couscous.

Quinoa and couscous are both easy to make, and they do not take long to cook. They are similar to making rice or pasta. You can find them in grocery stores in many places, in food co-ops, in large discount stores, and online. You can substitute them in most recipes here that call for rice or barley, if you like.

Recipe #7: Chicken and Melon

Prep time: 30 minutes; makes nine 1-cup servings

Ingredients:

3 lbs. skinless chicken, whole or pieces

1 medium sweet potato

8 oz. your dog's favorite pasta

1 cup cantaloupe (or other melon), cut up

½ cup plain, whole fat yogurt

Instructions:

Preheat oven to 350 degrees F. Lightly grease roasting pan.

Roast the chicken until the juices run clear when pierced with a fork or skewer. This usually takes 20 to 30 minutes for breasts or thighs; 45 to 60 minutes for a whole chicken. Allow the chicken to cool.

Roast the sweet potato with the chicken for about 25 to 30 minutes until soft. Allow the sweet potato to cool, then peel and cut up into smaller pieces.

Remove the bones from the chicken and cut the meat into large pieces.

Cook the pasta according to package directions.

Mix the chicken with the sweet potato and pasta, and top off with the cut up melon and yogurt.

Accompaniments:

Try adding some blueberries or cranberries to this recipe, or some sliced pears, to make your dog a real fruit cocktail with his dinner. Berries are full of antioxidants, along with vitamin C. Your dog does not need excessive amounts of vitamin C and his body can make its own, but a little extra from fresh berry sources can give his immune system a nice boost.

Tips:

You can make your own yogurt at home, if you start with good live active yogurt cultures. You need a candy thermometer to obtain accurate measurements; a large mixing bowl; a whisk for beating; and a sterilized glass container for the yogurt once it is made. It is important to use sterilized utensils and containers. Bacteria can ruin your yogurt and make it taste "off." You can sterilize your equipment by boiling it on the stove for a minute in a large pot, or by running clean equipment through the rinse cycle on your dishwasher.

You do not need to have a yogurt maker to make yogurt, but you do need a heat source. You can use a thermos, a wood stove, a heating pad, your oven, or even a crockpot. You will need whole milk and plain yogurt to get started.

To make yogurt using your oven, pour a quart of whole milk into a glass casserole dish. Add 3 tablespoons of plain, whole fat yogurt to the milk. The yogurt should state on the side that it contains active yogurt cultures. Stir the yogurt into the milk well and cover the casserole dish. Place the dish in a warm oven (100 degrees F) overnight with the heat turned off. Allow the milk and yogurt mixture to sit overnight. The active yogurt cultures in the yogurt will ferment with the milk overnight. You can allow it to sit in the oven for eight to ten hours. You can refrigerate in the morning.

The temperature must be between 100 and 110 degrees for the yogurt fermentation to occur so use your thermometer to check the temperature and make sure it is not too hot or too cold.

You can also obtain a yogurt starter culture from a health food store, if you prefer.

The recipes in this book call for whole yogurt instead of low-fat or fat-free yogurt because the good bacteria found in yogurt live in the fat content. The higher the fat content of the yogurt, the more good bacteria.

Recipe #8: Liver Lover's Dinner

Prep time: 20 minutes; makes eight 1-cup servings

Ingredients:

3 lbs. lean ground beef

8 oz. beef livers

1 cup canned pumpkin

1 medium apple, cut up

1 cup cooked, chopped
   green beans (or peas)

Instructions:

Cook ground beef in a pan over medium heat for about 15 minutes until the meat is brown and the juices run clear. Allow the meat to cool.

Simmer livers in a saucepan over medium-high heat with a small amount of water to cover them for about 20 minutes until they are cooked through. They should still be tender. Allow them to cool.

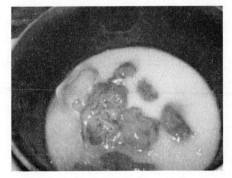

Cut up the livers into smaller pieces and mix them with the ground beef.

Mash up the canned pumpkin and mix it with the apple and green beans then add the vegetable mixture to the beef and liver mixture.

Accompaniments:

You can add a little garlic to this beef and liver meal, if you like. Some people swear by garlic. It has been used to keep fleas away, to boost the immune system, and even as a wormer for a long time. It is in the same plant family as onion, so some owners are afraid of using it because onion has been linked to autoimmune hemolytic anemia in dogs. It is your call, but a small amount of garlic in your dog's food once in a while will probably add some extra taste without doing any harm.

You can also add blueberries for taste, as seen in the picture at top of this recipe.

Tips:

Canned or puréed pumpkin is an old remedy for dogs with digestive problems. If your dog is constipated or has diarrhea, pumpkin can often help. It can bring stools back to the correct consistency. It is even safe enough for puppies to eat. If you are giving your dog pumpkin due to digestive upsets, your dog does not need much. A tablespoon is usually enough for a small to medium dog. Some dogs just love pumpkin though. The next time you have a Halloween pumpkin, do not toss it out the day after Halloween. Instead, you can put it in your oven on a low temperature and bake it for your dog. Cut it up in slices and your dog will enjoy having pieces of it as a snack. You can also scoop out the sides of the pumpkin (not the stringy parts or the seeds) and use them as filling for delicious pies.

When you are buying canned pumpkin in the grocery store, notice that there is a difference between canned pumpkin, the vegetable, and pumpkin pie filling. It is fine to give your dog canned pumpkin. It is not fine to give your dog pumpkin pie filling which contains nutmeg and other spices your dog does not need to eat, at least not in big helpings.

Recipe #9: Tuna Casserole

Prep time: 15 minutes; makes eight 1-cup servings

Ingredients:

> 2 lbs. tuna, canned in oil
>
> 2 cups baked potato, cut up
>
> 2 Tbsp. olive oil
>
> 1 cup grated carrots
>
> 4 Tbsp. plain, whole milk yogurt

Instructions:

Do not drain tuna; use the oil from the canned tuna in the meal.

Preheat oven on 350 degrees F. Prepare a casserole dish.

Mix the tuna, oil from the tuna can, the cut-up baked potato, olive oil, and grated carrots together. Spread in a casserole dish and place in the oven for ten to 15 minutes.

Remove tuna casserole from oven and allow to cool. Top with yogurt.

Accompaniments:

This dish is good with some nuts as a topping. You can use peanuts, almonds, or other nuts your dog likes. No macadamia nuts: they are toxic to dogs.

Tips:

You can use fresh tuna for this recipe if you prefer. If you use fresh tuna, bake the fish for ten to 15 minutes at 350 degrees F until the tuna starts to flake easily. Be sure to remove the bones from the fish before continuing with the recipe.

Canned tuna in oil gives good results for the casserole, but do not use canned tuna in water. The fat content in tuna canned in water is too low for most dogs.

When you prepare potatoes for dogs, be sure to inspect them for green spots. Green spots on potatoes are an indication of solanine, a natural toxin that occurs in some foods. Your dogs should not eat potatoes that have green spots. Potatoes are also not recommended for dogs that have arthritis or other joint problems.

Recipe #10: Salmon and Rice

Prep time: Ten minutes; makes six 1-cup servings

Ingredients:

   2 lbs. canned salmon

   1 cup brown rice

   1 cup broccoli, puréed

   ½ cup plain, whole milk yogurt

Instructions:

Do not drain salmon; use the oil from the canned salmon in the meal.

Cook the rice according to package directions.

Mix together the salmon, the rice, and the broccoli.

Top off the meal with the yogurt on the salmon mixture.

Accompaniments:

You can top off this recipe with some alfalfa sprouts as greens. They are a great source of trace minerals for your dog and they go well with the salmon. You can also add some dill and parsley for flavor.

Tips:

You can use salmon fillets for this meal if you prefer. If you use fresh salmon you will need to poach it for 15 to 20 minutes until it flakes. Then cool and remove the bones before proceeding with the recipe. You do not need to worry about removing bones from canned salmon. The fish is pressure cooked before canning and the bones are so soft they will not harm your dog.

Recipe #11: Favorite Salmon Dinner

Prep time: 20 minutes; makes six 1-cup servings

Ingredients:

- 2 lbs. canned salmon
- 1 medium sweet potato
- 1 cup cooked, chopped
    green beans
- 1 cup brown rice

½ cup plain, whole fat yogurt

Instructions:

Do not drain salmon; use the oil from the canned salmon in the meal.

Bake the sweet potato at 350 degrees F for about 30 to 45 minutes until soft. Allow to cool. Peel and remove the skin, then cut up into smaller pieces.

Cook the rice according to package directions.

Mix together the salmon in oil, the diced sweet potato, the green beans, and the rice.

Top off with yogurt over the mixture.

Accompaniments:

Chopped almonds are a nice topping for this recipe, as seen in the picture at the top of this recipe.

Tips:

As with other salmon recipes, you can use salmon fillets for this meal if you prefer. If you use fresh salmon you will need to poach it for 15 to 20 minutes until it flakes. Then cool and remove the bones before proceeding with the recipe. You do not need to worry about removing bones from canned salmon. The fish is pressure cooked before canning and the bones are so soft they will not harm your dog.

In most recipes, salmon, tuna, and jack mackerel are interchangeable. See what is on sale at your local store, or look and see what you might have in your kitchen cabinets, unless, of course, your dog has a preference for a certain kind of fish.

Recipe #12: Mackerel Dinner

Prep time: 15 minutes; makes six 1-cup servings

Ingredients:

- 2 lbs. canned jack mackerel
- 1 medium sweet potato
- 1 cup cooked, chopped green beans
- 2 cups plain, whole milk yogurt
- 2 Tbsp. fresh dill, chopped

Instructions:

Do not drain mackerel; use the oil from the canned mackerel in the meal.

Bake the sweet potato at 350 degrees F for about 30 to 45 minutes until soft. Allow to cool. Peel and remove the skin, then cut up into smaller pieces.

Mix together the mackerel, the sweet potato, and the green beans.

Mix the dill with the yogurt and spread on top of the mackerel mixture.

Accompaniments:

Pecans are a great accompaniment to the ingredients in this recipe. Chop a few and sprinkle them on top.

Tips:

You can use mackerel fillets for this recipe if you prefer, but be sure to use jack mackerel and not king mackerel because of the mercury content in king mackerel. If you use fresh mackerel you will need to bake it at 350 degrees F for about 15 minutes until it starts to flake easily. Allow it to cool and then carefully remove the bones. You do not need to remove the bones from canned fish because the fish is pressure cooked and they are so soft they will not harm your dog.

Recipe #13: Scrambled Eggs and Mackerel

Prep time: 25 minutes; makes six 1-cup servings

Ingredients:

2 lbs. canned mackerel

1 cup cottage cheese

4 eggs

½ cup cooked peas

3-4 slices canned peaches in natural juice

Instructions:

Do not drain mackerel; use the oil from the canned mackerel in the meal.

Mix together the cottage cheese, the peas, and the peach slices.

Lightly beat together the eggs to make scrambled eggs and cook them in a pan over medium-high heat for about six minutes until they are no longer runny.

Turn the scrambled eggs into the cottage cheese and peach mixture.

Top with the mackerel.

Accompaniments:

Add some apple or diced pears to this recipe to give it an extra fruity taste.

Tips:

As with the other mackerel recipes, you can use fresh mackerel if you prefer. If you do, be sure to use jack mackerel and not king mackerel because of the mercury content. To cook, follow the instructions in the last recipe.

Recipe #14: Salmon and Pasta

Prep time: 15 minutes; makes eight 1-cup servings

Ingredients:

   2 lbs. canned salmon
   1 lb. of your dog's favorite pasta
   ½ cup cooked, chopped green beans
   1 cup grated carrots
   ½ cup plain, whole milk yogurt
   3 Tbsp. chopped fresh dill

Instructions:

Do not drain salmon; use the oil from the canned salmon in the meal.

Cook the pasta according to package directions.

Mix together the green beans, the carrots, the yogurt, and the chopped dill.

Mix the salmon with the pasta.

Turn the vegetable and yogurt mixture in with the salmon and pasta mixture. Ready to serve.

Accompaniments:

Top with a little Parmesan cheese.

Tips:

In recipes that call for you to use pasta, you can use any kind of pasta your dog likes or anything you like. It is usually a good idea to steer clear of spaghetti as dogs may drop it on the floor and it can be messy. But smaller kinds of pasta such as ziti, pastina, corkscrew pasta, bowtie pasta, and pasta that comes in various shapes are all fine. Many dogs can eat these smaller kinds of pasta neatly.

Recipe #15: Cheese Omelet

Prep time: 20 minutes; makes five 1-cup servings

Ingredients:

   8 eggs

   8 oz. Cheddar cheese

   1 medium sweet potato

   1 cup fresh spinach, torn

   1 cup plain, whole milk yogurt

Instructions:

Lightly beat together the eggs to make scrambled eggs and cook them in a pan over medium-high heat for about five minutes until they are no longer runny. Allow them to cool.

Grate the Cheddar cheese and mix it in with the scrambled eggs.

Bake the sweet potato at 350 degrees F for about 30 to 45 minutes or until soft. Allow to cool. Peel and remove the skin, then cut up into smaller pieces.

Mix the sweet potato pieces into the scrambled eggs and cheese mixture.

Mix the spinach and yogurt together and add them to the sweet potato and scrambled eggs mixture.

Accompaniments:

If your dog likes fruit, consider dicing a pear and adding it to these scrambled eggs. Or add another fruit he likes such as some peach slices.

Tips:

This recipe is high in fat due to all of the Cheddar cheese. You can reduce the amount of cheese in the recipe if you are concerned about your dog's weight.

Recipe #16: Beef and Sweet Potato

Prep time: 20 minutes; makes seven 1-cup servings

Ingredients:

2 lbs. ground beef

4 oz. liver

1 ½ cups puréed sweet potato

8 oz. plain, whole milk yogurt

Instructions:

Cook ground beef in a pan over medium heat for about 15 minutes or until the meat is brown and the juices run clear. Allow the meat to cool.

Simmer livers in a saucepan over medium-high heat with a small amount of water to cover them for about 20 minutes until they are cooked through. They should still be tender. Allow them to cool.

Cut up the livers into smaller pieces and mix them with the ground beef.

Add the sweet potato to the beef and liver mixture.

Mix the yogurt with the beef and sweet potato mixture.

Accompaniments:

You can add some additional vegetables to this meal or add a different vegetable in place of the sweet potato if your dog prefers something else, zucchini for example.

Tips:

You can add brown rice or pasta to this dish to change it up.

Recipe #17: Chicken and Cottage Cheese

Prep time: 30 minutes; makes seven 1-cup servings

Ingredients:

2 lbs. chicken, whole or in pieces

¼ lb. beef kidneys

2 eggs

12 oz. of cooked cabbage and zucchini

½ cup cottage cheese

Instructions:

Preheat oven to 350 degrees F. Lightly grease roasting pan.

Roast the chicken until the juices run clear when pierced with a fork or skewer. This usually takes 20 to 30 minutes for breasts or thighs; 45 to 60 minutes for a whole chicken. Allow the chicken to cool.

Remove the bones from the chicken and cut the meat into large pieces.

Simmer beef kidneys in a saucepan with a small amount of water for about 20 minutes until they are thoroughly cooked. Allow them to cool.

Cut up the kidneys into smaller pieces and mix them with the chicken.

Beat the two eggs lightly and pour them in a pan over medium-high heat. Cook for about five to ten minutes until they are no longer runny.

Add the cabbage and zucchini mixture to the scrambled eggs.

Add the scrambled eggs to the chicken and kidneys. Mix together well. Top with the cottage cheese.

Accompaniments:

You can top this dish with some Cheddar cheese if you like.

Tips:

Many dogs are somewhat lactose intolerant, which is why it is not a good idea to give your dog whole milk. However, most dogs can eat dairy products such as cottage cheese, yogurt, and Cheddar cheese without any problems as they have less lactose in them than milk. If you notice that your dog has any gastric problems, it could be attributable to the dairy products.

You can substitute canned salmon or other fish for the chicken in this recipe, or use turkey, lamb, beef, or ground pork. You can also use other vegetables.

Recipe #18: Chicken Stew

Prep time: 30 minutes;
makes six 1-cup servings

Ingredients:

2 lbs. chicken, dark meat with
    skin, stewed

½ lb. beef liver

6 cups enriched egg noodles

½ cup carrots

¼ cup celery

Instructions:

Roast the chicken until the juices run clear when pierced with a fork or skewer. This usually takes 20 to 30 minutes for breasts or thighs; 45 to 60 minutes for a whole chicken.

Add the carrots and the celery to the chicken during the last 20 minutes of cooking. Allow the chicken and vegetables to cool.

Remove the bones from the chicken and cut the meat into large pieces.

Simmer beef liver in a saucepan with a small amount of water for about 20 minutes until they are thoroughly cooked. Allow them to cool.

Cut up the liver into smaller pieces and mix them with the chicken.

Cook the egg noodles according to the package directions.

Add the liver to the chicken. Mix well.

Add the mixture to the egg noodles. Mix thoroughly.

Accompaniments:

You can add a little garlic to this recipe if you like. It is usually safe to add half or one small clove per 20 pounds of your dog's weight.

Tips:

This recipe is basically a stew for dogs, or chicken and dumplings. It is fairly irresistible. The skin adds fat to the recipe and gives it a lot of flavor, but you can cook it without the skin if your dog is watching his weight.

Recipe #19: Beef and Rice

Prep time: 20 minutes; makes ten 1-cup servings

Ingredients:

2 lbs. lean ground beef

¾ lb. beef livers

3 ½ cups brown rice

1 cup cooked zucchini

1 cup cooked cauliflower

Instructions:

Cook ground beef in a pan over medium heat for about 15 minutes until the meat is brown and the juices run clear. Allow the meat to cool.

Simmer livers in a saucepan over medium-high heat with a small amount of water to cover them for about 20 minutes until they are cooked through. They should still be tender. Allow them to cool.

Cut up the livers into smaller pieces and mix them with the ground beef.

Cook the brown rice according to package directions.

Add the brown rice to the beef and liver mixture. Stir well.

Add the zucchini and cauliflower to the beef and rice mixture. Mix thoroughly.

Accompaniments:

You can top this dish with some nuts or berries, such as pecans and blueberries, or anything you and your dog like.

Tips:

This dish works with lots of different kinds of vegetables. Try adding some torn spinach to it for a nice change.

Recipe #20: Doggy Quiche

Prep time: 40 minutes; makes 1 dozen full-sized muffins or 2 dozen mini muffins

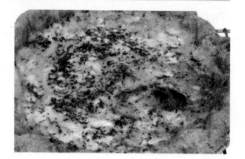

Ingredients:

> 1 cup oat flour
>
> ½ cup oat bran
>
> 2 eggs
>
> 1 lb. lean ground beef
>
> 1 cup spinach leaves, tightly packed
>
> 1 cup puréed carrots

Instructions:

Preheat oven to 400 degrees F.

Cook ground beef until the juices run clear.

Purée carrots in food processor. Purée spinach leaves in food processor separately.

Line a mini muffin pan with cupcake papers. You can also use a regular muffin pan to make full-size muffins.

Combine all of the ingredients together and mix thoroughly. Spoon mixture into cupcake papers nearly to the top and spread evenly.

Bake for ten to 15 minutes if you are using the mini muffin pan; bake for 20 to 25 minutes if you are using a regular muffin pan. The muffins are done when you can insert a toothpick into the center and pull it out cleanly.

Remove from the oven and allow to cool completely on a wire rack. Store in an airtight container in the fridge.

Accompaniments:

Try sprinkling some Cheddar cheese on top of these meaty muffins to complete the quiche comparison.

Tip:

Although this meat dish is baked in a muffin pan, it is not actually a muffin. If you feed your dog several of these "meat muffins," they should be quite filling and can be given as dinner.

Recipe #21: Turkey Balls

Prep time: 35 minutes;
this recipe makes a varying number
of balls depending on how big you
make them

Ingredients:

   1 ½ cup oat flour
   1 ½ cup brown rice flour

1 cup oat bran

1 cup sweet potatoes, mashed

1 cup raw, ground turkey (not turkey sausage)

1 egg

½ cup water

Instructions:

Preheat oven to 350 degrees F. Cook the sweet potatoes and mash them.

Line a cookie sheet with aluminum foil for easier cleanup.

Combine all of the ingredients together and mix them until they form a dough. Make the dough into small balls (the size of a golf ball) and place them on an ungreased cookie sheet.

Bake for 22 to 27 minutes or until the turkey balls begin to turn golden brown. Remove and allow to cool on a wire rack.

If you make the turkey balls smaller or larger, you will need to adjust the baking time.

Store in an airtight container in the fridge.

Accompaniments:

You can give these turkey balls to your dog as treats or as part of his dinner. The nice thing about them is that you can control how many of them you feed.

Tips:

Freeze turkey balls and take them with you when you and your dog are traveling. They are easy to thaw in a refrigerator, and you can give your dog as many of them as it takes to feed your dog a meal.

Recipe #22: Doggy Meatballs

Prep time: 35 minutes; this recipe makes a varying number of meatballs depending on how big you make them

Ingredients:

2 lbs. ground beef or turkey

½ cup grated Parmesan cheese

½ cup oat bran

1 tsp. dried parsley

¼ tsp. garlic powder (optional)

1 egg

Instructions:

Preheat oven to 350 degrees F.

Line a cookie sheet with aluminum foil for easier cleanup.

Combine all of the ingredients together and mix them until they form a dough. Make the dough into small balls (the size of golf balls) and place them on an ungreased cookie sheet.

Bake for 15 to 20 minutes or until the meatballs are browned all over. They should be thoroughly cooked. Remove and allow to cool on a wire rack.

If you make the meatballs smaller or larger, you will need to adjust the baking time.

Store in an airtight container in the fridge.

Accompaniments:

You can give these meatballs to your dog as treats or as part of his dinner. You can also serve them over pasta or vegetables.

Tips:

This recipe will work well with ground lamb or ground pork. You can also try using different grated cheeses.

Recipe #23: Broccoli and Chicken Balls

Prep time: 35 minutes; this recipe makes a varying number of balls depending on how big you make them

Ingredients:

1 cup oat flour

1 cup brown rice flour

½ cup oat bran

1 cup ground chicken, cooked

1 cup broccoli, puréed

1 egg

½ cup water

Instructions:

Preheat oven to 350 degrees F. Purée broccoli in food processor.

Line a cookie sheet with aluminum foil for easier cleanup.

Combine all of the ingredients together and mix them until they form a dough. Make the dough into small balls (the size of golf balls) and place them on an ungreased cookie sheet.

Bake for 22 to 27 minutes or until the chicken and broccoli balls are browned all over. They should be thoroughly cooked. Remove and allow to cool on a wire rack.

If you make the chicken balls smaller or larger, you will need to adjust the baking time.

Store in an airtight container in the fridge.

Accompaniments:

You can give these chicken balls to your dog as treats or as part of his dinner. Try adding a little Cheddar cheese to the chicken balls as a topping. They go well with the broccoli.

Tips:

You can use turkey or other poultry in this recipe. You can also make substitutions for the broccoli and use different vegetables.

Recipe #24: Salmon Patties

Prep time: 50 minutes; makes four 1-cup servings

Ingredients:

>   1 ½ cup tapioca or amaranth flour
>
>   8 oz. plain, whole milk yogurt
>
>   12 oz. canned salmon

Instructions:

Preheat oven to 350 degrees F. Empty salmon and juices into food processor and purée.

Line a 9 x 9 inch square pan with aluminum foil for easier cleanup.

Combine all of the ingredients together and thoroughly mix. Pour mixture into baking pan.

Bake salmon mixture for 30 to 40 minutes. Remove from oven and allow to completely cool on wire rack. Slice with a knife into individual portions. Store in an airtight container in the fridge.

Accompaniments:

These patties are great on their own, but you can also add some vegetables. Purée a cup of spinach and add it as a sauce, for example.

Tip:

You can use tuna or Jack mackerel instead of salmon in this recipe.

The recipes included in this chapter are basic meals for healthy dogs. Many of them can be modified for dogs that have allergies or other health issues by changing the meat or changing or omitting the carbs. All of the recipes presented here are easy to prepare. They do not require a great deal of skill in the kitchen or kitchen gadgets. Try a few recipes and see how your dog likes them.

The next chapter will cover meals for special conditions. If your dog has allergies, digestive problems, needs to lose weight, or has some other health problems, here are some recipes that might help.

Chapter 6

Recipes For Special Conditions

Jn this chapter, you will find recipes for a wide range of conditions that are not covered by the standard healthy dog diet. The information provided here is accurate to the best of our knowledge and abilities, but this book is not a substitute for consulting with a veterinarian. If your dog has a health issue that needs to be addressed, please talk to a vet.

Puppies

Most nutritional experts advise owners to feed a good commercial puppy food during the puppy's first year. Calcium is always a concern when you are feeding a homemade diet, and it is absolutely essential that puppies receive the right amount of calcium and that the calcium-phosphorus balance is appropriate. For this reason, most people, even those who feed their other dogs a homemade diet, feed their puppies a commercial puppy food. Some breeders and owners feed puppies a good quality adult food or a food approved for "all life stages" to keep the protein and calcium levels slightly lower. This can keep puppies in some larger breeds from growing too fast, especially in breeds where hip dysplasia and other joint problems are a concern. Breeds such as Great Danes, for example, are usually fed an adult food from the time they are puppies to discourage rapid growth.

If you wish to feed your puppy a homemade diet, you can use the recipes in the previous chapter and instead of adding 800 to 1,000 miligrams of calcium per pound of food, you can add 1,200 to 1,500 miligrams of calcium per pound of food for your puppy.

Pregnancy

Contrary to what most people think, it is not really necessary to start overfeeding your dog as soon as she becomes pregnant. A female dog can continue to eat her normal diet for the first four to five weeks of pregnancy. By the fourth week, the puppies are no bigger than walnuts and the expectant mother does not need a lot of extra calories for fetal growth at this time.

Dogs often go off their feed, or stop eating, for a day or two about three weeks after they are bred. This is when the embryos attach themselves to the uterine lining. New hormones are released, and your dog might experience a little "morning sickness." But this will pass after a day or two. You could tempt her to eat during this time with some of her favorite foods, such as some baked chicken or some hamburger. Make one of her special meals. But do not be surprised if she is not hungry around week three.

After week five, your dog will begin eating more and you can slowly start to increase her portions. You can add some extra protein to her basic diet, but do not add any extra calcium. Additional calcium is a no prior to giving birth (called whelping) because it can cause a serious condition known as eclampsia. So, do not add any extra yogurt or dairy products to your dog's meals. Extra fish, chicken, beef, and other proteins are fine. Some scrambled and boiled eggs are also a good idea.

During the last week or so before your dog is due to deliver, she may start to lose her appetite depending on how many puppies she is carrying. If she has a large litter she might not have much room left for food. You can offer her several small meals per day to make sure she is getting enough to eat.

During and after delivery, you can offer her some vanilla ice cream (no chocolate). Ice cream is excellent as a pick-me-up. It contains a small burst of sugar for energy she will need during whelping. The calcium is also good for her at this time and will help keep her calm. You can also offer her some broth or some baked chicken, or anything else she will eat.

Do not be surprised if your dog does not feel much like eating for the first day after delivering the puppies. Some dogs are tired right after delivery. But you can offer her things to try to tempt her to eat. As the puppies begin to nurse she will start to get hungry. From this point on, you can feed her as much as she will eat, including plenty of calcium and dairy products. She will be feeding the puppies now, so give her all she wants for the next few weeks. She will let you know when it is time to wean the puppies. At that point, you can start cutting back her meals to their pre-pregnancy portion size.

Recipe #25: Weaning Formula

There are many good weaning formulas. Most breeders who have been breeding dogs for long have their own. Here is a popular weaning formula for puppies you can start giving them when they are three to four weeks old.

Prep time: five minutes; makes 1 pint

Ingredients:

8 oz. goat milk

8 oz. plain, whole milk yogurt

2 egg yolk

2 Tbsp. mayonnaise (not salad dressing)

Instructions:

Combine all of the ingredients. The milk and yogurt should not be too cold or the puppies will not like the formula, but they do not need to be heated. You can place in a flat puppy pan or a "flying saucer" type pan, made to keep puppies from falling in, but puppies will likely get soaked the first time or two they try the formula.

As the puppies get a little older and start to use their teeth more, you can thicken the formula with rice baby cereal or begin directly adding some ground commercial puppy food. Eventually, you will be feeding the puppies more commercial food and less formula by the time they are about seven weeks of age. As already mentioned, most canine nutritionists recommend that young puppies start out eating a commercial diet to make sure they get the proper balance of calcium and phosphorus so important for growing puppies. You can begin changing their diet to homemade food once they have achieved their adult growth.

Tips:

You can buy canned goat milk in most grocery stores now. Goat's milk is similar, nutritionally, to dog milk. You can also use fresh goat milk if you know someone with a goat. Goats are quite popular as pets, and if you have a source for goat's milk, you can use it in some of your dog's meals. It makes a wonderful cheese.

Senior Dogs

Ideas about feeding senior dogs have been changing recently. At one time, it was believed that senior dogs should be fed lower protein diets in order to protect their kidneys. Today, most experts agree that it is not only all right for senior dogs to eat plenty of protein, unless they have a diagnosed problem with their kidneys, but that senior dogs actually need more protein than younger adult dogs. Dogs are prone to losing muscle mass as they age, and giving your senior dog additional protein can help him keep his muscles and stay better toned.

You can feed your senior dog all of the recipes in Chapter 5 for healthy adult dogs unless he has some other health problem that would indicate he should not eat them.

Some senior dogs do put on weight as they age, usually because they are leading a sedentary lifestyle. Help your dog stay fit by making sure he continues to get regular exercise each day, even if it is just a short walk. Light to moderate exercise will also aid in your dog's digestion. If you are concerned about your dog's weight, you can reduce some of the cheeses in the recipes; do not include skin in chicken or turkey recipes; and drain off the oil from the recipes that feature canned fish such as salmon, tuna, and jack mackerel.

Other senior dogs have the opposite problem: They start to lose weight as they get older. Some of these dogs may not have a hearty appetite. A senior dog's senses can start to dull with age, including his senses of smell and taste. Homecooking does a lot to keep a dog interested in his food, but you might still have to make your senior dog's meals as interesting as possible. Make sure his food is warm and that it smells good. Try adding some bacon to his meals. It is hard for any dog to resist bacon, and the smell is strong. If your dog is still not tempted to eat, have your veterinarian check his teeth. In some cases a dog will not eat because he has a bad tooth or other dental problem. Fixing the problem can quickly restore his appetite.

If your senior dog has trouble holding his weight, add a few extra carbs to his meal in the form of sweet potatoes. They are highly nutritious and are also strongly anti-inflammatory for dogs with arthritis problems. You can also add some pasta to your dog's meals for extra carbs.

You can add some extra fat to your senior dog's diet by including the skin on chicken and turkey, adding some extra cheese to his meals, and adding a little salmon oil to his diet. Fish oil, especially salmon oil, can provide health benefits for your dog, such as improved skin and coat, and salmon oil seems to provide even more benefits than ordinary fish oil. Both fish oil in general and especially salmon oil are high in calories, which can be good for a senior dog that needs to gain weight.

Many senior dogs also have problems with arthritis and joint pain. If your dog is affected by these issues, you may want to look into supplements such as glucosamine and chondroitin, which you can add to your dog's meals after they are prepared. The omega-3 fatty acids in fish such as tuna and salmon can also help your dog's arthritis.

Overweight Dogs

It is estimated that between 25 and 40 percent of dogs in the United States today are either overweight or obese. Many owners do not even realize that their dogs are overweight. If your dog could stand to lose a few pounds, there are some good recipes that will help your dog lose weight. If your dog does need to lose weight, you can help him cut calories by not giving him the skin from chicken or turkey, which contains lots of calories. Reduce carbs in your dog's diet. If your dog indicates that he's still hungry, you can add vegetables to his meals such as green beans, which help your dog feel full without adding a lot of calories. Cut down on snacks or try to feed healthy snacks such as carrots, apple slices, and popcorn (unbuttered, of course). Snacks and treats contain calories, too. They should not make up more than 15 percent of your dog's total caloric intake each day.

Recipe #26: Chicken and vegetables

Prep time: 15 minutes; makes six 1-cup servings

Ingredients:

6 oz. cooked chicken, diced

4 oz. zucchini

12 oz. chopped, cooked green beans

2 potatoes, baked, peeled, and chopped

4 oz. cooked brown rice

2 Tbsp. olive oil

4 Tbsp. plain, whole milk yogurt

Instructions:

Sauté potato in olive oil over medium heat for about five minutes.

Add the zucchini to the potatoes and cook slightly, then add the green beans.

Cook the rice following package directions.

Combine all of the vegetables with the rice and stir.

Add the cooked chicken to the vegetable and rice mixture and cook for another two minutes.

Add the yogurt to the chicken and vegetable mixture and stir through. Reduce heat to lowest setting and cook mixture, stirring constantly. Cover the pan with a lid and cook for another five minutes. Allow to cool.

Accompaniments:

You can top this recipe with some peanuts if you like.

Tips:

Green beans are filling. You can make many recipes "diet" meals for your dog by cutting down on some of the other ingredients and adding some green beans. Just be careful you do not reduce your dog's protein intake too much.

Recipe #27: Beef pasta

Prep time: 25 minutes; makes 11 1-cup servings

Ingredients:

2 lbs. lean ground beef

3 cups mixed green vegetables (broccoli, zucchini, peas) puréed or steamed

2 cups of your dog's favorite pasta

16 oz. can of diced tomatoes

2 Tbsp. tomato paste

Instructions:

Cook the ground beef in a pan over medium-high heat for about five to ten minutes or until it is done and the juices run clear.

Add the green vegetables to the ground beef and cook together for about five minutes.

Cook the pasta following the package directions.

Add the diced tomatoes and the tomato paste to the ground beef mixture and bring to a boil. Bring the mixture to a boil and then simmer for another ten minutes. Stir occasionally.

Add the pasta to the ground beef mixture and stir thoroughly. Allow to cool before serving.

Accompaniments:

What else? Add some Parmesan to this delicious pasta dish for your dog. But go easy: this recipe is for dogs that need to lose weight.

Tips:

You can use any vegetables your dog likes in this recipe, but purée them or steam them before adding them to the meat. Dogs are able to digest vegetables much more easily if they have been partly broken down before they eat them.

Fruits are a great source of fiber for your dog's diet without adding calories.

Recipe #28: Lean but not mean meal

Prep time: 25 minutes; makes nine 1-cup servings

Ingredients:

    2 lbs. venison
    3 cups cooked green beans, chopped
    1 cup canned pears in juice, chopped
    1 cup grated carrots

Instructions:

Preheat oven to 350 degrees F. Lightly grease a roasting pan.

Cut the venison into large pieces and place in the roasting pan. Use a meat thermometer in one of the pieces of venison if you have one.

Roast the venison for about 25 minutes or until the meat thermometer shows a temperature of 165.

Add the carrots to the venison five minutes before you take the venison out of the oven to cook them.

Take the venison and carrots out of the oven. Allow to cool.

Mix the green beans and pears together. Then mix the green beans and pears with the venison and carrots. Ready to serve.

Accompaniments:

Add some cranberries to this dish for a little extra pizzazz. They are tart and fruity and will go well with pears. They are also high in antioxidants and good for your dog.

Tips:

Venison is a "novel" protein, or one your dog does not encounter normally unless you go out of your way to make it part of his diet. It is usually a good idea to stick to feeding your dog the proteins he is used to eating, such as chicken, beef, lamb, and others that you see often. That way if he should develop an allergy to one of these proteins, it will be easy to switch him to a protein he has not had before. However, venison is low in fat, and if your dog needs to lose weight, it is a meat you might want to consider.

Recipe #29: Chicken and fruit

Prep time: 30 minutes;
makes ten 1-cup servings

Ingredients:

> 3 lbs. chicken, whole
>> or in pieces
> 8 oz. chicken livers
> 1 cup canned peaches in
>> natural juice
> 1 cup canned pears in natural juice
> 1 cup plain, whole milk yogurt

Instructions:

Preheat oven to 350 degrees F. Lightly grease roasting pan.

Roast the chicken until the juices run clear when pierced with a fork or skewer. This usually takes 20 to 30 minutes for breasts or thighs; 45 to 60 minutes for a whole chicken. Allow the chicken to cool.

Remove all the bones from the chicken and cut the chicken into large pieces.

Simmer the livers in a saucepan covered by a small amount of water over medium-high heat for about 20 minutes until they are thoroughly cooked. They should still be tender, but not falling apart. Allow them to cool.

Drain the peaches and pears. You can add the natural juices to the meal if you prefer, but it will make the meal soupier.

Cut the livers into smaller pieces and mix them with the chicken pieces. Add the peaches, pears, and yogurt to the chicken and livers. Serve.

Accompaniments:

You can add some honey to top off this recipe.

Tips:

This recipe is relatively low in fat. You can make it lower by using light meat chicken instead of dark meat. Dark meat has more calories.

Keep in mind that many of the recipes in Chapter 5 will work for dogs trying to lose weight if you adjust them by cutting down on the cheese or draining off the oil from the fish. Increase the vegetables and fruits and cut down on the carbs, and many meals can help your dog lose a little weight.

Dogs with Food Allergies

Although the number of dogs with food allergies is relatively low in the U.S., if you happen to have such a dog, it is a serious problem. There are also dogs that have food intolerances, which can be just as hard to deal with as allergies.

Dogs can be allergic to many different food ingredients, or more than one thing. If your dog is showing symptoms of having a food allergy, it is important for you to work with your veterinarian to determine what your dog is allergic to so you can change your dog's diet to something he can tolerate.

Symptoms of food allergies may include:

- Allergy symptoms that continue year-round
- Ear infections
- Hot spots
- Itching, especially around the face, paws, ears, arm pits, forelegs, stomach, and tail
- Loss of hair
- Recurring skin infections
- Scratching
- Sometimes more frequent bowel movements

Symptoms of food intolerances:

- Diarrhea
- Vomiting

The ingredients most likely to cause an allergic reaction in dogs are, in order:

- beef
- dairy products
- chicken
- lamb
- fish
- eggs (from chickens)
- corn
- wheat
- soy

Your vet will likely ask you and your dog to go through a feeding trial to pinpoint what your dog is allergic to. The first phase is an elimination diet. During this time you will feed your dog a single protein and a single kind of carbohydrate. You will need to keep your dog on this diet for 12 weeks. That means no snacks, treats, no doggy toothpaste with other ingredients, nothing else. Just those two ingredients you know your dog can tolerate. You will need to make sure you choose two ingredients your dog is not allergic to. This may mean using a protein and carbohydrate your dog has never eaten before, such as a novel protein (kangaroo anyone?). This is why experts urge dog owners not to feed their dogs novel proteins for meals on a random basis. They need to save those novel proteins for situations such as feeding trials and elimination diets.

If you are feeding your dog a novel protein your dog has never eaten before, your dog should not be allergic to it. A dog (or a human) has to be exposed to an allergen more than once in order for the body to develop an allergic response to the protein that triggered the allergy. So, if your dog has never eaten a particular kind of protein before, he should not have any allergic response to it, at least at first. It is possible that your dog may become allergic to the novel protein, however, but it would take a while for this to happen.

During this time, you and your vet will observe whether your dog's symptoms clear up. This will confirm that your dog has a food allergy. After this phase, if your dog's symptoms have cleared up, your vet will ask you to "challenge" your dog by giving him things from his previous diet. If his symptoms return, you will know which ingredients in the food were caus-

ing the allergy and you can start eliminating some of those ingredients and put your dog on a new diet.

If your dog's symptoms do not clear up, it means that he is allergic to something in the food you are feeding him, which could be either the novel protein or the carbohydrate. Your dog might have previously been exposed to the novel protein. Or you may need to confirm that your dog has an allergy and not some other problem. You and your vet will need to start over.

It is hard to suggest substitutions for dogs with allergies because every dog is different. However, here are some substitutions you might be able to make if your dog has allergies:

Gluten-Free Flour Mix I

¼ cup soy flour
¼ cup tapioca flour
½ cup brown rice flour

Gluten-Free Flour Mix II

6 cups white rice flour
2 cups potato starch
1 cup tapioca flour

If your dog is allergic to wheat, soy, or corn, of course, you will need to avoid foods that contain those ingredients.

There are many possible substitutions for eggs. If you require an egg replacement that binds, you can use tomato paste, mashed sweet potatoes, mashed potatoes, arrowroot powder, or potato starch. Use 2 to 3 tablespoons of one of these ingredients instead of an egg.

Other Egg Replacement Options

- 1 egg = ¼ cup canned pumpkin or squash
- 1 egg = 2 Tbsp. water + 1 Tbsp. oil + 2 tsp. baking powder
- 1 egg = 1 Tbsp. ground flax seed simmered in 3 Tbsp. water
- 1 egg white = 1 Tbsp. plain agar powder dissolved in 1 Tbsp. water, whipped, chilled, and whipped again

You will find some good recipes below for dogs with food allergies. There are some novel proteins included, as well as some gluten-free meals for dogs who have problems with gluten.

Recipe #30: Tasty duck

Prep time: 30 minutes; makes 12 1-cup servings

Ingredients:

3 lbs. skinless duck, whole or in pieces, light and dark meat

2 cups sweet potatoes

8 oz. duck livers

8 oz. your dog's favorite pasta

2 medium apples, cored and diced

Instructions:

Preheat oven to 350 degrees F. Lightly grease roasting pan.

Roast the duck (the breast will take 20 to 30 minutes; an entire duck will take 45 to 60 minutes). The duck is done when the meat juices run clear when pierced with a skewer.

Roast the sweet potatoes with the duck for the last 25 to 30 minutes or until they are soft. Allow to cool.

Simmer the duck livers in a pan over medium-high heat with a small amount of water for about 20 minutes. Cook them until they are thoroughly done, but do not overcook. They should be firm but not falling apart. Allow to cool.

Cook the pasta according to package directions.

Remove all the bones from the duck and cut the meat into large pieces.

Cut the livers into smaller pieces and mix with the duck, the pasta, and the apple pieces.

Accompaniments:

Try adding some cranberry sauce to top off this recipe.

Tips:

Duck is a novel protein, as most dogs do not eat it unless you make a point of giving it to them. It makes a good meat protein for a dog with allergies unless your dog is allergic to poultry in general. Duck is, however, expensive, as are many of the novel proteins. It is also a little fattening, so it is good for a dog that needs to gain weight. Many dogs with food allergies do need to add some weight.

If your dog is allergic to wheat or does not do well with the carbs in pasta, you can omit the pasta in this recipe.

Recipe #31: Buffalo and barley

Prep time: 20 minutes; makes 11 1-cup servings

Ingredients:

　　3 lbs. buffalo meat

　　1 cup oatmeal

1 cup barley

1 cup canned peaches, in natural juice

1 cup canned pears, in natural juice

1 cup fresh spinach leaves, torn

Instructions:

Cook the buffalo meat in a pan over medium heat for about 15 minutes until the meat is brown and the juices run clear.

Cook the oatmeal and barley according to package directions.

Mix the oatmeal and barley together and add the buffalo meat.

Cut up the fruit and add it to the buffalo mixture. Stir in the spinach.

Accompaniments:

You can add a little molasses to this dish to tie all of the ingredients together.

Tips:

Buffalo meat is much leaner than beef, and most dogs have not eaten it. It is a novel protein for them. You can substitute beef in this recipe if your dog is not allergic to it.

Recipe #32: Buffalo stew

Prep time: 45 minutes; makes 12 1-cup servings

Ingredients:

3 lbs. ground buffalo meat

2 cups sweet potatoes, diced

½ cup peas

½ cup carrots, chopped

½ cup cooked green beans, chopped

2 medium apples, cut up

Instructions:

Cook buffalo meat in a pan over medium-high heat for about 20 minutes until done and the meat juices run clear. Allow to cool.

Bake the sweet potato at 350 degrees F for about 30 to 45 minutes, or until soft. Allow to cool. Peel and remove the skin and mash.

Mix the mashed sweet potatoes with peas, carrots, and green beans.

Add the apples to the sweet potato mixture.

Add the buffalo to the vegetable mixture. Serve.

Accompaniments:

You can add spinach to this recipe if your dog likes it.

Tips:

You can use ground buffalo or buffalo meat cut into chunks for this recipe. Venison or other novel meat proteins will also work in place of the buffalo. Ostrich or emu meat is also available in some stores or online. Rabbit is another novel protein for many dogs, and it costs less than many other novel proteins. You may be able to find a rabbit breeder in your area who can supply you with fresh rabbit.

This recipe is also gluten-free.

Recipe #33: Lamb and rice

Prep time: 20 minutes; makes nine 1-cup servings

Ingredients:

   3 lbs. lamb, ground or chunked

   3 eggs

   ½ cups peas

   1 cup brown rice

   1 cup canned peach slices, in natural juice

Instructions:

Cook lamb in a pan over medium heat for about 15 minutes until it is no longer pink and the juices run clear. Allow to cool.

Cook the rice according to the package directions.

Scramble the eggs in a pan over medium heat for about five minutes until they are no longer runny.

Mix the lamb with the scrambled eggs and allow the mixture to cool.

Add together the peas, the rice, and the peaches, then mix in the lamb and egg mixture. Serve.

Accompaniments:

Add some mint or berries to this recipe for some additional flavor.

Tips:

In the old days, 20 to 25 years ago, lamb was still a novel protein and it was not found often in commercial dog foods. If you had a dog that had allergies, your vet would suggest to you to cook lamb and rice on a daily basis for your dog. Times have changed. Today lamb and rice dog food is on every pet store shelf. But if you would like to cook your own lamb and rice meal for your dog, this is a good recipe, without gluten, and lamb is less likely to trigger food allergies than beef or chicken.

Recipe #34: Chicken and sweet potatoes

Prep time: 30 minutes; makes ten 1-cup servings

Ingredients:

3 lbs. skinless chicken

2 medium sweet potatoes

8 oz. chicken livers

1 cup peas

Instructions:

Preheat oven to 350 degrees F. Lightly grease a roasting pan.

Roast the chicken until the juices run clear when pierced with a fork or skewer. This usually takes 20 to 30 minutes for breasts or thighs; 45 to 60 minutes for a whole chicken. Allow the chicken to cool.

Add the sweet potatoes to the chicken 25 to 30 minutes before it is done. Allow to cool. Peel and dice.

Remove all the bones from the chicken and cut the chicken into large pieces.

Simmer the livers in a saucepan covered by a small amount of water over medium-high heat for about 20 minutes or until they are thoroughly cooked. They should still be tender but not falling apart. Allow them to cool.

Cut the livers into smaller pieces and add them to the chicken, sweet potatoes, and peas.

Accompaniments:

Add some peaches or other fruit to this recipe to make it a little sweeter for your dog.

Tips:

This recipe is also gluten-free, though it contains plenty of protein and fiber, and sweet potatoes are high in carbohydrates. If your dog does not like peas, you can substitute another vegetable such as zucchini, squash, cauliflower, broccoli, or anything else your dog likes. Just remember that some vegetables are harder for your dog to digest, so steam them or purée them before adding them to your dog's meal.

Dogs with Bad Breath

It is not unusual for dogs to have bad breath. Many dogs like to eat things that taste bad. You can improve your dog's breath by brushing your dog's teeth on a weekly basis with doggy toothpaste. Meals like the ones provided here will also help, which feature mint and parsley, two herbs known for making breath smell nicer.

If your dog's breath is persistently bad, ask your vet to take a look at your dog's teeth. Your dog could have a bad tooth or another dental problem that needs repair. You can give your dog these meals at any time, as

part of his normal diet. You can also add mint and parsley to other meals to help improve your dog's breath. Apples are also good for your bad breath, and raw carrots are good for your dog's teeth.

Recipe #35: Cure for bad breath meal

Prep time: 30 minutes; makes nine 1-cup servings

Ingredients:

3 lbs. skinless chicken, light and dark meat

2 cups sweet potatoes, cut up

1 cup plain, whole milk yogurt

2 Tbsp. fresh mint, chopped

2 tsp. fresh parsley, chopped

Instructions:

Preheat oven to 350 degrees F. Lightly grease a roasting pan.

Roast the chicken until the juices run clear when pierced with a fork or skewer. This usually takes 20 to 30 minutes for breasts or thighs; 45 to 60 minutes for a whole chicken. Allow the chicken to cool.

Add the sweet potatoes to the chicken 25 to 30 minutes before it is done. Allow to cool. Peel and dice.

Remove all the bones from the chicken and cut the chicken into large pieces.

Add the sweet potatoes to the yogurt, mint, and parsley.

Mix the sweet potato mixture together with the chicken. Serve.

Accompaniments:

Add a little honey to this recipe to bring out the sweetness of the sweet potatoes.

Tips:

Try to use fresh herbs for this recipe, especially if you are making it to improve your dog's breath. The fresh herbs will be more intense than dried herbs and do much more to freshen your dog's breath.

Recipe #36: Turkey and rice

Prep time: 45 minutes; makes nine 1-cup servings

Ingredients:

> 3 lbs. skinless turkey pieces, light and dark meat
>
> 2 Tbsp. fresh parsley, chopped
>
> 1 cup cooked green beans, chopped
>
> 1 medium apple, diced
>
> 1 cup brown rice

Instructions:

Preheat oven to 350 degrees F. Lightly grease a roasting pan.

Roast the turkey pieces until the juices run clear when pierced by a fork or skewer. This usually takes 30 to 45 minutes for a boneless breast or thigh; 45 to 60 minutes for a breast or thigh with bone; and one and a half to two hours for an entire turkey, depending on its size.

Remove all of the bones from the turkey and cut the meat into large pieces.

Cook the brown rice according to the package directions.

Add the parsley to the turkey pieces and then mix the turkey with the green beans, apple, and brown rice.

Accompaniments:

Consider adding some cranberries or other berries to this recipe.

Tips:

The parsley in this recipe is a good breath freshener for dogs with bad breath. Apples are also good for making the breath sweeter and more pleasant.

Recipe #37: Mint chicken

Prep time: 30 minutes; makes nine 1-cup servings

Ingredients:

3 lbs. skinless chicken, light and dark meat

2 Tbsp. fresh mint, chopped

1 cup cantaloupe (or other melon)

1 cup barley

½ cup peas

1 cup plain, whole milk yogurt

Instructions:

Preheat oven to 350 degrees F. Lightly grease a roasting pan.

Roast the chicken until the juices run clear when they are pierced with a fork or skewer. This usually takes 20 to 30 minutes for breasts or thighs; 45 to 60 minutes for a whole chicken. Allow the chicken to cool.

Remove all the bones from the chicken and cut the chicken into large pieces.

Cook the barley according to the package directions.

Add the mint to the melon.

Mix the chicken and the peas with the barley, then add the chicken and barley mixture to the melon. Top with the yogurt.

Accompaniments:

Sprinkle with blueberries to top off the meal.

Tips:

Mint leaves are excellent for improving your dog's breath. It is often used for human breath fresheners such as toothpastes, mouthwashes, and dental flosses. Never use human toothpaste or dental products for your dog. They contain a substance called xylitol, which is an artificial sweetener that can be toxic to dogs.

Herbs from the mint family also aid digestion.

Digestive Problems

Dogs can have digestive problems for many of the same reasons people do. Your dog might eat some food that is spoiled, or he could have a mild case of food poisoning. There might be an ingredient in his food that disagrees with him and causes a temporary stomach upset. Your dog could pick up something he should not and eat it when you take him to the dog park. Your dog could have an upset stomach if you make a sudden change in his diet. Or your dog could be recovering from an illness or infection that could include vomiting and/or diarrhea. All of these digestive problems are usually temporary in nature.

New dog owners may be surprised to learn that it is not unusual for dogs to vomit or have diarrhea. It does not always mean that your dog is seriously ill. A dog may eat some grass to make himself vomit to get rid of something bad he has eaten, for example. Some dogs will produce a foamy vomit if they go too long between meals. You do not need to rush your dog to the vet if your dog vomits occasionally. However, if your dog is vomiting continuously, or if the vomiting continues more than a day, you should take your dog to the veterinarian. Your dog could become dehydrated, and your vet should determine what is causing the problem.

The same is true with diarrhea. Many dogs will have an occasional bout of diarrhea. It is usually nothing to be too concerned about as long as it does not last more than a day or so. You can give your dog a tablespoon of canned pumpkin to help stop the diarrhea. But remember that if your dog has diarrhea, it can mean that your dog's body is trying to get something out of his body that has disagreed with him in some way. You can give your dog's body a few hours to try to handle the problem on its own. If your dog is still having diarrhea after a day, or if he is having stools that contain any blood or black, tarry-looking matter, then take him to the vet right away.

The recipes provided here for digestive problems are intentionally bland. When your dog is vomiting or having diarrhea, the last thing you want to do is give him anything to eat that could further irritate his stomach. These recipes are meant to be used temporarily when your dog's stomach is upset. Once your dog is no longer vomiting or having problems with diarrhea, he should be able to return to his normal diet unless your veterinarian advises you to make some changes. Avoid feeding foods with much fat or dairy, as they could cause more problems with diarrhea. Keep your dog's food simple while he is recovering.

Recipe #38: Low-fat chicken broth

Ingredients:

3 chicken leg quarters

Distilled water

Instructions:

Remove skin from whole chicken or chicken pieces. You can use three leg quarters in a pressure cooker and remove the skin before cooking. Place the chicken in the pot with distilled water. For the pressure cooker, cook on high for two hours; in a stock pot simmer on low heat for 16 to 24 hours.

Remove the chicken and bone from the broth and discard or save to use in another recipe once your dog is feeling better. All the nutrients are in the stock.

Pour the broth into a fat separator (looks like a pitcher with the spout coming from the bottom.) After ten minutes the fat will float to the top. Pour off the small amount of fat at the top and pour the low-fat broth into a container.

Refrigerate the broth. When the broth is cold, any fat remaining will be gelatin on the top. You can remove it, or you can pour all of it through a super fine mesh strainer, which will stop the fat and allow the plain broth through.

Tips:

You can use low fat chicken broth for dogs that need a low-fat and low-phosphorus diet as well. It is best not to add any salt or seasoning to this broth.

Recipe #39: Bad tummy meal

Prep time: 30 minutes; makes 11 1-cup servings

Ingredients:

4 lbs. skinless chicken or lean ground beef

2 cups brown rice

1 cup applesauce

Instructions:

Cook the chicken (or beef) in a pan with a little water over medium heat for about 15 minutes until it is completely cooked. Drain. Allow to cool.

Cook the rice about 15 minutes longer than the package directions state.

Shred the chicken, or crush the beef into tiny pieces.

Completely mix the meat with the rice and add the applesauce into the mix.

Accompaniments:

If your dog is able to eat it, you can add a little yogurt to this mix.

Tips:

This basic recipe, using chicken and rice, or beef and rice, is an old-time favorite for treating a dog with an upset tummy. It is often the first thing a dog can eat if he has been vomiting or if he has had diarrhea. The applesauce is optional, but it will help your dog's stomach if he can keep the mixture down.

Dogs with Kidney Problems

At one time research seemed to indicate that dogs with kidney disease should be fed a low protein diet, but current research indicates that is not necessary unless your dog has seriously impaired kidneys. If 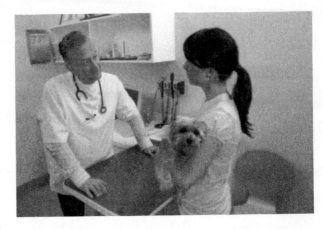 your dog has early to moderate kidney disease, see a vet for treatment and advice about what he can eat. Your dog should eat a diet that is greatly reduced in phosphorus, though it can be higher in fat. The protein your dog eats need to be good quality meat protein. It can come from any animal as long as it uses good quality parts. And, your dog needs to drink as many liquids as possible, so stews and foods that have liquids in them are good. If your dog has kidney problems, he should avoid foods high in phosphorus such as pumpkin and squash, cheese, nuts, flax seeds, and soybeans.

Recipe #40: Lamb and kidneys

Prep time: 20 minutes; makes seven 1-cup servings

Ingredients:

2 lbs. lamb

1 ½ cups sweet potatoes, boiled and diced

4 egg

4 egg whites

4 oz. lamb kidneys (or other kidney)

½ cup plain, whole milk yogurt

Instructions:

Cook lamb in a pan over medium heat for about 15 minutes until it is no longer pink and the juices run clear. Allow to cool.

Remove the lamb from the pan and cut it into large pieces.

Scramble the eggs, including the egg whites, in a pan over medium-high heat for about five minutes until they are no longer runny. Allow to cool.

Cook the kidneys in a pan over medium heat with a small amount of water for about 15 minutes until they are thoroughly cooked. They should still be tender but not falling apart. Allow to cool.

Add the lamb to sweet potatoes. Add the kidneys to the scrambled eggs. Fold the kidneys and scrambled eggs into the lamb mixtures. Top with the yogurt.

Accompaniments:

If you prefer, you can reduce some of the sweet potatoes in this recipe and include some green beans or some white rice instead. You can add some butter to this recipe for your dog to increase the fat level without increasing the phosphorus.

Tips:

This recipe is designed for dogs with kidney problems. It is relatively high in fat and low in phosphorus. It still has plenty of protein in it so it is not for dogs that cannot eat protein at all, but if your dog can eat moderate amounts of protein, this recipe should be fine. You can also substitute beef with higher amounts of fat instead of the lamb. If lamb kidneys are hard to find, you can use chicken or beef livers in this recipe.

Egg whites are pure protein, which means you can add them to the recipe and keep the phosphorus level lower than if you add more whole eggs.

CASE STUDY: FEEDING A DOG WITH CHRONIC RENAL FAILURE
Sandy Beaudoin

Sandy Beaudoin has been homecooking for her dog for almost two years.

I originally decided to switch my dog to a homecooked diet because of the lack of availability of a prepared food that met the dietary requirements that I wished to provide my dog with his problems. My dog has Chronic Renal Failure (the slow loss of kidney function over time) combined with Fanconi Syndrome (a disorder of the kidney tubes in which certain substances normally absorbed into the bloodstream by the kidneys are released into the urine instead), but that is pretty exclusive to Basenjs.

The basics of his diet are a good meaty protein and glutinous rice. I use all available meats; beef, pork, turkey, chicken, venison (when I can get it), bison (when I can afford it), etc. Eggs are also a staple, particularly powdered egg whites to raise the protein level with a minimum of phosphorus. To the basic protein and rice, I add a vegetable or fruit, also rotated among those that he will eat; green beans, beets, carrots, sweet potatoes, white potatoes, peas, pumpkin, applesauce, stewed tomatoes, etc. Fats (bacon fat, salt free butter, coconut oil) and sometimes other carbohydrates (pasta in various forms, tapioca, barley) are used when needed to reach the desired calorie count. All the meat is human grade purchased at my local stores.

I am using an Excel spread sheet to help maintain a diet of high protein and low phosphorus for a dog in Chronic Renal Failure. I build my recipes through the use of a spreadsheet developed for creating meals for animals in various stages of CRF, with guidelines with regard to amounts of protein to feed and phosphorus limitations. The nutrition numbers for various foods were gathered from **www.nutritiondata.com** plus a few other resources with regard to raw foods. The spreadsheet makes it quite easy to substitute various ingredients and immediately see the nutritional differences and allow for corrections.

He likes some recipes more than others. He has always been a dog that would eat any food ravenously for a few days, then go off it completely, so it is difficult to tell. I don't think he likes it any better than commercial food, but his running mate certainly does! I have to completely isolate them from each other at feeding time or she would eat all of his first. He is maintaining his overall condition very well. In spite of having two severely debilitating problems, he weighs more than he ever has in his life and has not changed his "lifestyle" one iota.

I usually devote one day to cooking for him about every two weeks. I cook in what amounts to four-day batches, divided into single meals, and freeze. All my recipes are developed by weight, so it is easy to figure a single meal's worth. I never cook less than three batches, which is about two week's worth, and sometimes I have cooked as many as six batches, which would be a minimum of 24 days. It takes anywhere from two to four hours each cooking day. I now make "meatloaf" nearly every time, so baking time must be considered.

I always recommend homecooking to people with CRF dogs. I personally believe commercially available "kidney" diets contain very poor quality in general and not enough protein to maintain a truly healthy animal. As for advice I would offer to others thinking of homecooking, remember, with regard to general nutrition and micro-elements, the mantra is "balance over time." Don't beat yourself up trying to create the perfect meal every day. Rotate both major and minor ingredients from day to day or batch to batch. You don't eat a perfect nutritionally balanced meal every time you eat, and neither does your dog.

The biggest rewards of homecooking are a healthy, happy dog and knowing you are doing the best you can for a creature that is dependent upon you for all their basic needs.

Diabetic Dogs

Diabetic dogs generally need to eat a diet that is higher in protein and fiber and lower in carbohydrates and fats to keep their blood glucose levels stabilized. Dog usually do well on diets with increased fiber. If you have a dog that is diabetic, it is important that you put your dog on a good schedule and feed him at regular mealtimes. Small meals, often, will help. He should also get regular exercise. And, if he is overweight, as many diabetic dogs are, then you should talk to your veterinarian about carefully helping him lose weight. Many dogs with diabetes need to eat extra fiber to help them absorb carbohydrates and reduce the glucose in their bloodstream.

If your dog is diabetic, he needs to avoid eating high amounts of sugars and simple carbs, as opposed to more complex carbs, which take longer to digest. Avoid fatty meats that can stress the pancreas, though some fat in the diet is necessary. Choose grains that are healthier for your dog, such as brown rice and oats. Vegetables and fruit are still good for your dog.

Recipe #41: Beef and barley

Prep time: 20 minutes;
makes 12 1-cup servings

Ingredients:

   3 lbs. lean ground beef

   2 ½ cups barley

   2 ½ cups brown rice

   1 cup celery, chopped

Instructions:

Cook ground beef in a pan over medium heat for about 15 minutes until juices run clear. Allow to cool.

Cook barley according to package directions.

Cook rice according to package directions.

Add beef and celery to barley and rice. Mix thoroughly. Serve.

Tips:

You can use other vegetables instead of the celery, such as green beans or spinach. Different lean meats instead of beef will also work in this recipe, such as skinless chicken.

Recipe #42: Beef and vegetables

Prep time: 60 minutes; makes 15 1-cup servings

Ingredients:

    3 lbs. lean beef, cubed
    1 ½ cups carrots
    1 cup celery
    1 bunch broccoli
    ½ cup spinach
    1 ½ cup whole grain rye
    2 cups brown rice
    8 oz. beef broth

Instructions:

Cook the beef in the beef broth and some water for about 20 minutes until it is thoroughly cooked. It should be tender but not falling apart. Remove from the pan and allow to cool.

Add the rye to the pan and simmer for 40 minutes.

Add the rice to the rye and simmer for 15 minutes. Turn off heat and let sit.

Mix the carrots, celery, broccoli, and spinach together with the beef.

Add the rice and rye to the meat and vegetable mixture and mix thoroughly.

Accompaniments:

You can add lots of things to this recipe, including garlic, if you like.

Tips:

You can use any kind of lean ground meat or beef for this recipe. And you can use lots of different vegetables. The recipe works because the brown rice is a complex carbohydrate, which is okay for diabetic dogs to have. The meat is high in protein and there is lots of fiber in this recipe, but it is low in fat.

IBD Diets

IBD or inflammatory bowel disease is not well understood in dogs, and the exact cause is not known. This makes treating the disease somewhat difficult. Part of managing IBD is managing your dog's diet.

In order to confirm that your dog has inflammatory bowel disease, your vet will probably put your dog on a hypoallergenic diet and ask you and your dog to go through the same kind of food trial that dogs suspected of having food allergies go through. Your dog will be restricted to eating one protein and one carbohydrate he has not eaten before. Or the diet could use hydrolyzed proteins. Hydrolyzed proteins are proteins that have been broken up into such minute particles that a dog's immune system does not recognize what kind of protein they were originally, so there is no reaction to them.

With IBD, every dog is different. Some dogs are able to tolerate diets that are low in fat. Some dogs need a diet that is low fiber. And some dogs with have colon problems may need a diet that is high in fiber. Homemade diets are often used, but they are usually developed in consultation with a veterinary nutritionist to make sure they are not lacking anything that particular dog needs in his diet.

There is no sample recipe for the IBD diet, but your dog may benefit from eating meals that are low in fat and avoiding grains.

Breed-Specific Diet Requirements

Some breeds may have specific dietary requirements. However, the majority of breeds and individual dogs will do well eating a healthy variety of meats and other ingredients as described in these chapters. If you have concerns about your dog's diet or your dog does not seem to be thriving on the kinds of meals described here and in other books on the subject, then consult with a veterinary nutritionist who can assess your individual dog to see if he is missing some important vitamins or minerals in his diet.

Most dogs have the same nutritional requirements. The exceptions would cover issues like the need for giant breed dogs to be particularly careful about their calcium intake because of their rapid growth and inclination toward hip dysplasia; or for Labrador Retrievers to have their weight gain carefully monitored. These are breed proclivities but if you feed a generally healthy diet and watch your dog's condition your dog should be fine.

Chapter 7

Portions — How Much and How Often?

hat you feed your dog, in terms of proteins, fats, carbs, vitamins, and minerals, is important. The ingredients provide your dog with the nutrition he needs. However, owners often overlook another crucial element in feeding their dogs: managing their dog's portions.

A sizable number of dogs in the United States are overweight or obese today, and the cause is usually due to overfeeding. Owners often blame commercial diets for their dogs becoming overweight because many commercial foods contain high percentages of grains and carbohydrates. However, even dogs that are fed a homemade diet can become overweight if owners do not feed the correct portions.

Overweight and obese dogs can suffer from diabetes mellitus, respiratory disease, heart problems, arthritis, joint problems, digestive disorders, and other health problems. And their lives can be shortened.

How Much to Feed?

In order to determine how much to feed your dog on a homemade diet, you need to know how much your dog weighs, assuming he weighs close to his ideal weight and you want to feed him a maintenance diet. The meals provided in Chapter 5 will suit a dog on a maintenance diet.

In Chapter 3, you will find the table Average Daily Energy Needs. You can check the table to find out how many calories your dog needs per day. So, if you have a dog that weighs 50 pounds, he will need 1,353 calories per day. If your dog is less active, he will need fewer calories. And if he is a working dog that gets much more exercise, he will need more calories.

How do you translate this information into knowing how much home-made food to feed your dog? You can check the calorie information for any food you plan to feed your dog on the USDA calorie charts at **www.nal. usda.gov/fnic/foodcomp/Data/SR17/wtrank/sr17a208.pdf**. These are 30 pages of comprehensive information about foods and the calories they contain. You can also look at the serving size information provided for recipes you intend to follow. Perhaps the simplest rule to follow for know-ing how much food to feed your dog is to feed him 2 to 3 percent of his body weight per day. So, if your dog weighs 100 pounds, you would feed him 2 to 3 pounds of food per day. If he weighs 50 pounds, you would feed him 1 to 1 ½ pounds per day. (It does help to have a calculator sometimes if you are feeding your dog a homemade diet.)

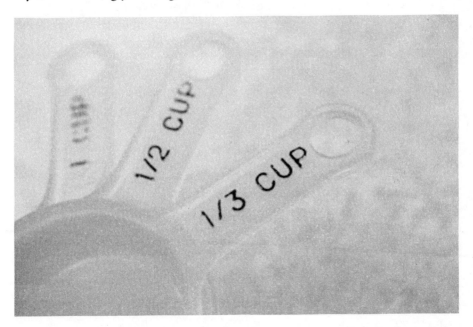

Growing puppies need to eat about 10 percent of their body weight per day.

It is also important for you to watch your dog's weight and condition. No matter what the tables say or how many calories you feed, you see your dog everyday. If your dog seems to be losing weight when he should not, you should feed him more food. If he is gaining too much weight, then cut back on his portions. There is no substitute for what you observe with your own eyes.

CASE STUDY: A HANDY WAY TO USE LEFTOVERS

Ginger Corley

I've had dogs all my life, and I've been cooking for them probably the last 25 years (I'm 53 now). I've always given them leftovers and bought them goodies at the grocery store, but that was when I finally bought them their own crock pot and started making my batches of "dog stew."

The dogs eat a basic diet of kibble plus about ¾ to 1 cup of dog stew each day. You never know what the stew will contain. There are some basics such as a meat source. I frequently will buy chicken gizzards and hearts at the grocery store for starters, then start adding things from there.

There is no specific diet. I have a crock pot that always has some sort of "dog stew" in it though really it's more of a soup. It contains some sort of meat, and after that you never know. Because I cook for only one human, it makes it easy to dispose of my own leftovers. So there may be vegetables, fruit, or just about anything in there. If I hard-boil eggs, I drain the water into the crock pot. If I open a can of fruit, I drain the juice into the crock pot. So the dog stew changes from day to day and even from one meal to the next. I don't use recipes. Other than minor things, such as if I see that one has loose stools I will add a can of pumpkin, there are no recipes.

My dogs all seem to have cast iron stomachs. I think that because I feed them such a variety of foods from the time they are in utero (as a breeder, most of my dogs were conceived and born in my own home) until they pass away, they develop a tolerance that they wouldn't have if they were only fed one variety of one manufacturer's kibble. Where food and gastrointestinal issues are concerned, knock on wood, I've not run into problems in my personal dogs.

I think they have more robust health because they are always eating a variety of foods. Wouldn't you get bored if you ate the same thing with every meal, every single day? It also makes them less prone to upset stomach if something changes in their kibble. They are already used to their dog stew changing every day, so a change in kibble is merely a trifle. I think my dogs are healthier because of the homecooking. They have better coats and virtually no stomach problems for multiple generations. Plus, my dogs all have great appetites. I never have a picky eater or even a slow eater. Most of all, I think the dogs just plain like it, and I think it is an economical way to dispose of my scraps and leftovers.

The thing that takes the longest is probably cleaning the crock pot out between batches, and that really is only a couple minutes at the most. Once it's cleaned, I toss in the meat that I'm starting with, some water, and usually some seasonings — sage and ginger are the most common — and set it to begin cooking. That's it. It takes maybe two to three minutes.

I frequently recommend the dog stew/crock pot method to friends and have gotten a number of people who are now using it rather than buying canned food. It is far less expensive.

My advice to others thinking of homecooking would be to buy a separate crock pot so you can keep it going even when you want to cook something for yourself. And shop for it in a thrift shop. Plus, hand out soup bones (beef knuckle bones) on a regular basis. Since I started giving them to my dogs at least once a week, I have not had to clean the teeth of any of them. That is a huge relief after having to clean the teeth of my mutt every year for all 15 years of her life.

It can be hard to keep the food on hand in sufficient quantities when you are feeding a quantity of dogs. I don't have a separate freezer, and the one with my refrigerator is so small that I barely have room for my own food. While I was building the house I'm in now, I had to live in an apartment for six months and my dogs rotated in and out of a boarding kennel. I had to give up trying to keep dog stew going during this time because I didn't have enough dogs at the apartment to consume the big pots I was used to making. Instead, I gave them a lot of chicken wings and turkey necks and other raw meats, bones, and vegetables (most dogs LOVE carrots). But once we got moved into the new place and the crock pot was going, you could see them doing the big sigh of relief and saying, "we're finally home again."

How Often Should You Feed?

Once you have an idea of how much food your dog needs to eat each day, you will probably be wondering how often to feed him. This issue is not completely settled, and different people feed their dogs more or less during

the day. Young puppies should be fed three or four times per day, especially right after weaning. They can gradually transition to eating twice per day as they get a little older.

Adult dogs are usually fed twice per day, though some owners prefer to feed their dogs once per day. If you have a large, deep-chested breed that is prone to bloat, or gastric dilatation and volvulus, it is recommended that you feed your dog two or three times per day.

Bloat is a life-threatening illness that comes on suddenly without warning. With bloat, the stomach fills with gas or foam and then twists. The condition often needs to be treated with surgery, and it is often fatal. It is thought that feeding your dog several small meals per day can reduce the chances of the dog getting bloat if you have a breed that is susceptible to it, such as a German Shepherd, a Great Dane, or an Irish Setter.

Most dogs will do well on 1 or 2 meals per day. If you feed your dog one meal per day, you might need to add some dog cookies as a pick-me-up if your dog has some down time between meals. Some dogs will vomit slightly between meals if they are only fed once a day because their stomach is too empty. Other dogs do well just eating one larger meal per day.

If you have a Toy breed, then it is usually best to feed two or three small meals per day as some Toy breeds can be prone to hypoglycemia. Several small meals will keep them from having ups and downs with their blood sugar.

Depending on how many meals you plan to feed your dog per day, you will need to divide the total amount of food per day for your dog by the number of feedings and spread them out accordingly.

 Free Feeding

Some owners like the idea of free feeding. Free feeding, also called self-feeding, is when you leave food down for your dog all the time and allow him to eat whenever he likes. Free feeding is convenient for the owner; however it is not usually a good idea when you are feeding a homemade diet because the food can spoil in the floor during the day. In addition, dogs that are allowed to free feed are often overweight. They tend to snack all day instead of leaving the food alone when they are no longer hungry.

Multiple Dogs

If you have one dog, then mealtimes might be easy for you. You only have to worry about whether your dog will like the food you have prepared. However, if you have multiple dogs, mealtimes might be a lot more exciting, to put things euphemistically. You may have to contend with dogs that growl, fight, or try to guard food. Feeding multiple dogs can be a circus. And that is especially true when you are feeding your dogs homemade meals they love.

If you have dogs that get into tussles at mealtime, the simplest way to keep things calm is by crating your dogs to feed them or feeding your dogs in separate rooms. Separating dogs at mealtimes means every dog gets their own food. No one fights. No one has to guard his dish. There is no growling. And each dog can eat at his own pace. You also do not have any dogs stealing food. This means you do not have one dog that weighs twice as much as the other dogs, while one poor dog is skinny, even if you never see the thief stealing the food. It takes a little coordination at first, but in just a few days your dogs will know where they are supposed to go to get their food and they will go there and be waiting for you. Mealtimes will be peaceful, the way they are supposed to be, and your dogs can enjoy their homemade food.

Chapter 8

Treats, Snacks, and Special Occasions

reats and snacks are an important part of life for most dogs and their owners. If you are committed to providing a healthy diet for your dog by cooking for him, you will also want to provide your dog with treats and snacks that are healthy. In this chapter, you will find tips on buying healthy treats for your dog as well as many recipes for making your own treats and cookies.

Buying Healthy Treats for Your Dog

Unlike dog food, treats, cookies, and biscuits do not need to be "complete and balanced" or nutritionally adequate as determined by AAFCO (the As-

sociation of American Feed Control Officials), which regulates standards for dog food. No one really expects a dog to depend on treats for his entire diet, so dog treats are not held to the same nutritional standards as dog food. While dog foods must either go through six-month feeding trials or show that their food is nutritionally balanced at least on paper, dog treats have a much easier time. You could feed your dog a diet of his favorite peanut butter cookies, but it would not be healthy for him.

With all that being said, however, commercial dog treats can still meet some of the minimum standards prescribed for dog foods. AAFCO's minimum standards are not especially high, so if you buy treats or cookies for your dog that carry an AAFCO approval that is a good start, but it does not necessarily mean the cookies are of exceptionally high quality. If you are looking for high quality treats for your dog then look for more than just the AAFCO seal of approval.

There are a number of good dog food treats on the market today that meet or exceed AAFCO's nutritional standards. There are also average and poor quality treats being sold. Some of the treats you find in stores may use terms such as "gourmet," "natural," or "holistic" to describe their products. You should be aware that in the world of dog food and dog treat labeling, these terms have inexact meanings. Advertising is advertising, even for dog treats, and these terms are often used to appeal to the consumer (you) even if they have no specific AAFCO meaning. There is nothing to prevent any manufacturer from using these terms to make their dog treats sound more appealing to you or to make you think they are better for your dog. Instead of relying on these terms to choose dog treats, read the labels for yourself just as you would your dog's regular food.

If you are looking for healthy dog treats, then look for treats that are as close as possible to what you would make in your own kitchen. Look for healthy ingredients such as natural peanut butter, pumpkin, liver, tuna, eggs, and carob. Look for whole wheat flour used as the base grain, as cookies require a batter or dough. Look for a natural preservative such as vitamin E. If you see an ingredient label that is full of chemicals and words you cannot pronounce, you are most likely not looking at a product with natural ingredients.

Keep in mind that dog treats are the equivalent of candy for your dog. You can look for healthy ingredients, but your dog's diet should not depend on what is in his treats or cookies.

Making Homemade Treats for Your Dog

When you are making homemade treats for your dog, pay close attention to the recipe, especially the amounts of dry and liquid ingredients. Cookies depend on keeping the right balance of dry to liquid so they turn out right according to the recipe, whether that is crisp or gooey. If you are recalculating a recipe, make sure you multiply or divide carefully to try to keep the proportions correct.

Some recipes may call for you to include liquid in other forms, for instance by puréeing liver or including the liquid from a can of tuna. Make sure you notice where you are supposed to do these things. If you do not follow these instructions, your recipe might not turn out well.

Many recipes will also allow you to mix and match. For instance, a recipe might call for tuna, but it is all right to substitute salmon or some other similar fish. Or, if a recipe calls for liver, you could reduce the liver and use some

egg in its place. If the recipe calls for one vegetable, you could use a different vegetable. It is fine to be creative when you are making treats for your dog — as long as you remember to keep the dry to liquid ratio used in the recipe.

Homemade dog treats usually fall into several categories. There are cookies that can be made with cookie cutters or dropped on a cookie sheet. There are loaf-type treats that can be baked to be soft. Some of these treats can then be sliced and given to dogs in this form. There are treats that can be baked until they are hard and treats that can be cooked in the microwave. And there are cakes and cupcakes for dogs. And, of course, there are treats that can be improvised, such as sliced hot dogs and popcorn, which make great training treats. There is virtually no limit to the ideas you can come up with for your dog.

Tips and Tricks for Making Dog Treats

Most dog treats are easy to make. They are not much harder than making cookies or biscuits for your family or friends. You may have to purée liver once in a while or drain a can of tuna, but other than that, the recipes are similar.

Here are a few tips and tricks for making dog treats that should help when it comes to cooking and baking.

1. Find out what your dog likes. It is always a good idea to bake things that will be appreciated, and it is no different when you are baking for your dog. If you know that your dog really loves bacon or cheese, look for recipes that contain those ingredients. If you know your dog does not care for garlic, leave it out of the recipes that call for it. There is no rule that says you have to follow a recipe exactly. By choosing recipes you are reasonably sure your dog will like, you are doing yourself and your dog a favor.

2. Before you begin cooking, make sure you have all of the cookware and ingredients you need. This will save you from having to stop in the middle of cooking to run out and get something. And we all know if you leave your ingredients on the counter, your dog is likely to eat them before you finish cooking them.

3. You can make dog cookies look nicer by cutting them out into dog biscuit shapes. It is not hard to find bone-shaped cookie cutters online or at pet supply stores. You can also find cookie cutters in the shape of dogs or other doggie items. Check kitchen supply stores and online kitchen sites. Your dog might not care, but they are cute. You might want to go to this extra trouble if you are giving the cookies as gifts or planning to have them at a doggie party.

   You can also cut out cardboard shapes of bones or dogs to use as guidelines when you cut shapes in the cookie dough.

4. You can make some dog treats more interesting by adding some Parmesan cheese to the tops of the treats. Most dogs love Parmesan, and it goes well with many recipes.

5. Keep in mind that many kinds of dog cookies freeze well, so it is easy to make a large batch at one time and freeze it. Try filling up a doggie treat bag with the just-baked cookies and popping it in the freezer, or fill up several treat bags. That way you will have treats ready for your dog whenever you need them.

6. You can also make easy treats for your dog by baking a piece of chicken and slicing it into small bits. Or, try slicing a hotdog into small bits and putting it in the microwave. These are both popular treats for dogs. Another good treat for dogs — and one that is easy to make — is baking a piece of liver on low in your oven (about 200 degrees F) for a couple of hours. Allow the liver to cook until it is dry and then cut it into small pieces. These liver bits make excellent training treats.

These tips will help you make treats and cookies your dog will love. Use your imagination and remember that your dog does not care if you give him hotdog bits or gourmet dog cookies. He just likes the treats you make for him.

A Word on Cookie Yields

It is difficult to give estimates regarding how many treats or cookies a recipe will make. The number of cookies a recipe yields always depends on what kind and size of cookie cutter you use. Most recipes for dog cookies are designed to make 2 to 3 dozen cookies using a 1 to 1 ½ inch cookie cutter. You can usually stretch a recipe to make more cookies if they are smaller, or make larger (but fewer) cookies.

Quick and Easy Dog Cookie Recipes

Making cookies for your dog does not have to mean spending hours in the kitchen slaving over a hot stove. There are lots of cookies you can make for your dog that only take about half an hour. These cookies are easy, and your dog will love them.

Recipe #43: Peanut butter and pumpkin dog treats

Prep time: 40 minutes

Ingredients:

2 ½ cups whole wheat flour

2 eggs

½ cup canned pumpkin

2 Tbsp. peanut butter

½ tsp. salt

½ tsp. ground cinnamon

Instructions:

Preheat oven to 350 degrees F.

Whisk together the flour, eggs, pumpkin, peanut butter, salt, and cinnamon in a bowl.

Add water as needed to help make the dough workable, but the dough should be dry and stiff.

Roll the dough into a ½-inch thick layer and then roll it up like a jelly roll. Cut into ½-inch pieces.

Bake in preheated oven until hard, about 40 minutes.

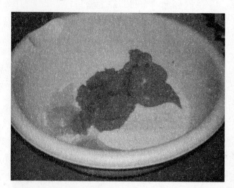 

Recipe #44: Minty breath cookies

Prep time: 35 minutes

Ingredients:

1 cup oat flour

1 cup brown rice flour

3 Tbsp. applesauce

½ cup dried mint

½ cup dried parsley

1 egg

¾ cup water

Instructions:

Preheat oven to 350 degrees F.

Combine all of the ingredients together and mix them until they form a dough. Roll them into small balls and place them on an ungreased cookie sheet.

Bake for 20 to 25 minutes. Remove and allow to cool on a wire rack.

Store in an airtight container in the fridge.

Recipe #45: Turkey gobble cookies

Prep time: 35 minutes

Ingredients:

    1 cup oat flour
    1 cup brown rice flour
    1 cup raw ground turkey (not turkey sausage)
    1 tsp. garlic powder (optional)
    1 egg
    ¾ cup water

Instructions:

Preheat oven to 350 degrees F.

Combine all of the ingredients together and mix them until they form a dough. Roll them into small balls and place them on an ungreased cookie sheet.

Bake for 20 to 25 minutes or until cooked completely through. Remove and allow to cool on a wire rack.

Store in an airtight container in the fridge.

Recipe #46: Deluxe tuna cookies

Prep time: 40 minutes

Ingredients:

  1 cup oat flour

  1 cup brown rice flour

  1 6-oz. can albacore tuna

  ¼ cup oat bran

  ¼ cup garlic powder (optional)

  1 egg

  ⅔ cup water

Instructions:

Preheat oven to 350 degrees F.

Empty contents from can of tuna, including juices, and purée in food processor.

Combine all ingredients, including puréed tuna, and mix together until a dough forms. Roll out onto a lightly floured surface to ¼ inch thickness. Use a cookie cutter or knife to cut into individual pieces.

Line cookie sheet with aluminum foil for easier cleanup.

Put tuna pieces on foil-lined cookie sheet and place in oven.

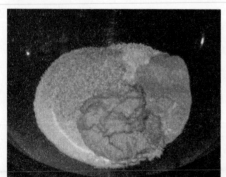
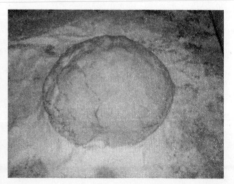

Bake cookies for 20 to 25 minutes. Remove and allow to cool on a wire rack. Store in an airtight container in the fridge.

Recipe #47: Special liver treats

Prep time: 40 minutes

Ingredients:

> 1 ½ cups tapioca flour (you can substitute amaranth flour
> > if you prefer)
> 1 lb. beef liver
> 2 eggs

Instructions:

Preheat oven to 300 degrees F.

Purée liver in a food processor. Clean up your food processor immediately afterward, as liver will dry and cake on it, and it can be hard to remove it later.

Combine all ingredients together and mix completely.

Line a loaf pan with aluminum foil to make for easier cleanup later.

Pour the liver mixture into the pan and bake for 30 minutes.

Cut the cooked liver into individual portions using a knife. Remove the pan from the oven and allow it to cool completely on a wire rack. Store in an airtight container in the fridge.

If you wish, you can leave the pan with the liver in it in the oven for about two more hours after slicing it, with the heat turned down to 150 degrees F. This will make the liver crunchy. Lots of dogs love to eat crunchy liver treats.

Recipe #48: Sweet potato cookies

Prep time: 45 minutes

Ingredients:

- 1 ½ cups oat flour
- 1 ½ cups brown rice flour
- 2 cups cooked, mashed
    sweet potatoes
- 1 cup oat bran
- 1 Tbsp. honey
- 1 egg
- ⅔ cup water

Instructions:

Preheat oven to 350 degrees F. Cook and mash the sweet potatoes. You can bake them or microwave them as you prefer. Put them in the food processor to make them smooth after cooking.

Combine all ingredients and mix together until a dough forms. Roll out onto a lightly floured surface to ¼ inch thickness. Use a cookie cutter or knife to cut into individual pieces.

Line cookie sheet with aluminum foil for easier cleanup.

Put the cookie pieces on foil-lined cookie sheet and place in oven.

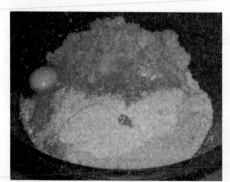

Bake cookies for 20 to 25 minutes. Remove and allow to cool on a wire rack. Store in an airtight container in the fridge.

Recipe #49: Pumpkin cookies

Prep time: 35 minutes

Ingredients:

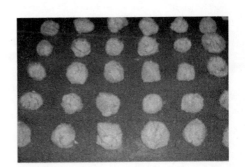

   1 ½ cups oat flour

   1 ½ cups brown rice flour

   1 cup canned pumpkin

      (or fresh puréed pumpkin)

   1 tsp. cinnamon

   1 egg

   ⅓ cup water

Instructions:

Preheat oven to 350 degrees F.

Combine all of the ingredients together and mix them until they form a dough. Roll them into small balls and place them on an ungreased cookie sheet.

Bake for 20 to 25 minutes. Remove and allow to cool on a wire rack.

Store in an airtight container in the fridge.

Recipe #50: Peanut butter cubes

Prep time: 10 minutes

Ingredients:

> 3 cups plain, whole milk yogurt
>
> 1 cup peanut butter
>
> 1 Tbsp. honey

Instructions:

Combine all of the ingredients together and use a whisk to mix together thoroughly. Pour mixture into ice cube trays and freeze in your freezer until solid (at least two hours). Pop them out and serve to your dog as an iced treat. You can give the cubes to your dog frozen, or you can soften them in the microwave first.

Recipe #51: Banana and pumpkin squares

Prep time: 45 minutes

Ingredients:

> 1 ½ cups oat flour
>
> 1 ½ cups brown rice flour
>
> 1 cup old-fashioned rolled oats
>
> 1 tsp. cinnamon
>
> 2 eggs
>
> ¼ cup vegetable oil
>
> ½ cup molasses, regular or blackstrap
>
> 2 cups pumpkin, canned or fresh
>
> 2 cups bananas, mashed and puréed

Instructions:

Preheat oven to 350 degrees F. Peel bananas, mash and purée in the food processor.

Lightly grease a 9 by 9 inch square baking pan.

Combine all of the ingredients until they are thoroughly mixed. Pour mixture into baking pan.

Bake mixture 30 to 35 minutes or until toothpick is clean when removed from center. The top should appear golden brown and the sides should begin to pull away from the sides of the pan.

Remove the pan from the oven and allow to cool completely on a wire rack. Slice into individual squares when cool. Store in an airtight container in the fridge.

Recipe #52: Peanut butter and carob cookies

Prep time: 35 minutes

Ingredients:

- 1 ½ cups oat flour
- 1 ½ cups brown rice flour
- ¼ cup carob powder
    (do not use chocolate)
- ½ cup carob chips (do not use chocolate chips)
- 1 egg
- ½ cup peanut butter
- 1 Tbsp. honey
- ⅔ cup water

Instructions:

Preheat oven to 350 degrees F.

Combine all of the ingredients together and mix them until they form a dough. Roll them into small balls and place them on an ungreased cookie sheet. Press each ball down to form a flat cookie.

Bake for 18 to 22 minutes or until the edges turn golden brown. Remove and allow to cool on a wire rack.

Store in a loosely covered container at room temperature.

Recipe #53: Peanut cookies

Prep time: 35 minutes

Ingredients:

1 ½ cups oat flour

1 ½ cups brown rice flour

½ cup finely chopped peanuts

½ cup old-fashioned rolled oats

2 eggs

¼ cup molasses, regular or blackstrap

½ cup peanut butter

½ cup water

Instructions:

Preheat oven to 350 degrees F.

Combine all of the ingredients together and mix them until they form a dough. Roll them into small balls and place them on an ungreased cookie sheet.

Bake for 18 to 22 minutes or until the edges turn golden brown. Remove and allow to cool on a wire rack.

Store in a loosely covered container at room temperature.

Recipe #54: Banana and oat cookies

Prep time: 35 minutes

Ingredients:

1 ½ cups oat flour
1 ½ cups brown rice flour
1 tsp. cinnamon
1 cup old-fashioned rolled oats
½ cup oat bran
1 egg
½ cup bananas, mashed and puréed
½ cup water

Instructions:

Preheat oven to 350 degrees F.

Combine all of the ingredients together and mix them until they form a dough. Roll them into small balls and place them on an ungreased cookie sheet. Press each ball down to form a flat cookie.

Bake for 18 to 22 minutes or until the edges turn golden brown. Remove and allow to cool on a wire rack.

Store in a loosely covered container at room temperature.

Recipe #55: Mock-choc cookies

Prep time: 40 minutes

Ingredients:

> 1 ½ cups oat flour
>
> 1 ½ cups brown rice flour
>
> 1 cup carob chips (do not use chocolate chips)
>
> 1 egg
>
> ½ cup peanut butter
>
> 1 cup water

Instructions:

Preheat oven to 350 degrees F.

Combine all of the ingredients to-gether except the carob chips and mix them until they form a dough. Roll them into small balls and place them on an ungreased cookie sheet. Press down on each ball with your thumb to form a small indented space in the center. Sprinkle a few of the carob chips into each indented space. They will melt when baking to form a delicious carob center. Leave space between these cookies. They will ex-pand.

Bake for 18 to 22 minutes or until the edges turn golden brown. Remove and allow to cool on a wire rack.

Store in a loosely covered container at room temperature.

You can also use these ingredients to make mock-chocolate chip cookies. Combine all of the ingredients together including the carob chips and mix them until they form a dough. Roll them into small balls and place them on an ungreased cookie sheet. Press them down to flatten them. Leave space between them. They will expand. Follow the rest of the directions above.

Recipe #56: Apple cinnamon cookies

Prep time: 35 minutes

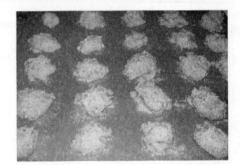

Ingredients:

- 1 ½ cups oat flour
- 1 ½ cups brown rice flour
- 2 ½ tsp. cinnamon
- ½ cup oat bran
- 1 egg
- ½ cup applesauce
- 2 Tbsp. honey
- 1 cup water

Instructions:

Preheat oven to 350 degrees F.

Combine all of the ingredients together and mix them until they form a dough. These cookies are hard to roll because they are so sticky, so you can use your spoon to scoop a small amount of dough and drop it on an ungreased cookie sheet to make drop cookies. The cookies do not spread when baked, so whatever shape you drop the dough is the shape they will have when baked.

Bake for 18 to 22 minutes or until the edges turn golden brown. Remove and allow to cool on a wire rack.

Store in a loosely covered container at room temperature.

Recipe #57: Peanut butter oatmeal cookies

Prep time: 35 minutes

Ingredients:

 1 ½ cups brown rice flour

 2 cups old-fashioned rolled oats

 1 egg

 1 cup peanut butter

 4 Tbsp. applesauce

 ¼ cup honey

 ⅛ cup water

Instructions:

Preheat oven to 350 degrees F.

Combine all of the ingredients together and mix them until they form a dough. Roll them into small balls and place them on an ungreased cookie sheet. Press each ball down to form a flat cookie.

Bake for 18 to 22 minutes or until the cookies begin to turn golden brown. Remove and allow to cool completely on a wire rack.

Store in an airtight container in the fridge.

Recipe #58: Deluxe oatmeal cookies

Prep time: 35 minutes

Ingredients:

 1 ½ cups oat flour

1 ½ cups brown rice flour

1 tsp. baking powder

½ tsp. baking soda

2 cups old-fashioned rolled oats

1 cup finely chopped peanuts

2 eggs

¼ cup vegetable oil

¾ cup peanut butter

½ cup honey

1 tsp. vanilla extract

Instructions:

Preheat oven to 350 degrees F.

Combine all of the ingredients together and mix them until they form a dough. Roll them into small balls and place them on an ungreased cookie sheet. Press each ball down to form a flat cookie.

Bake for 18 to 22 minutes or until the edges begin to turn golden brown. Remove and allow to cool completely on a wire rack.

Store in a loosely covered container at room temperature.

Recipe #59: Ginger cookies

Prep time: 35 minutes

Ingredients:

2 cups oat flour

2 cups brown rice flour

2 tsp. baking soda

2 tsp. ground ginger

1 tsp. cinnamon

1 egg

¼ cup vegetable oil

½ cup molasses, regular or blackstrap

1 cup water

Instructions:

Preheat oven to 350 degrees F.

Combine all of the ingredients to-gether and mix thoroughly. Spoon the mixture out and drop onto an ungreased cookie sheet. These cook-ies do not rise, flatten, or change shape when they bake, so if you want a flatter cookie, you should flatten it when you place it on the cookie sheet. You can also form the ginger cookies into shapes.

Bake for 18 to 22 minutes or until the edges begin to turn golden brown. Remove and allow to cool completely on a wire rack.

Store in a loosely covered container at room temperature.

Ginger cookies are good to give to dogs that have motion sickness or upset stomachs.

Recipe #60: Carob chip cookie

Prep time: 35 minutes

Ingredients:

1 ½ cups oat flour

1 ½ cups brown rice flour

1 cup carob chips (do not use chocolate chips)

1 egg

1 tsp. vanilla extract

1 cup water

Instructions:

Preheat oven to 350 degrees F.

Combine all of the ingredients together and mix them until they form a dough. Roll them into small balls and place them on an ungreased cookie sheet. Press each ball down to form a flat cookie.

Bake for 18 to 22 minutes or until the edges begin to turn golden brown. Remove and allow to cool completely on a wire rack.

Store in a loosely covered container at room temperature.

Recipe #61: Autumn cookies

Prep time: 50 minutes

Ingredients:

1 cup oat flour

1 cup brown rice flour

1 cup pumpkin, canned or fresh

2 Tbsp. molasses, regular
   or blackstrap

1 tsp. cinnamon

1 egg

Instructions:

Preheat oven to 350 degrees F.

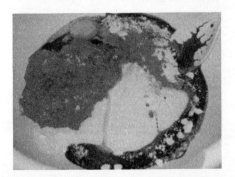

Combine all ingredients and mix together until a dough forms. Roll out onto a lightly floured surface to ¼ inch thickness. Use a cookie cutter or knife to cut into individual pieces. You can make the cookies follow a Halloween theme by using a pumpkin or spooky cookie cutters. Use a knife to cut out eyes or a scary mouth.

Line cookie sheet with aluminum foil for easier cleanup.

Put cookies on foil-lined cookie sheet and place in oven.

Bake cookies for 20 to 25 minutes. Remove and allow to cool on a wire rack. Store in an airtight container in the fridge.

Recipe #62: Double cheese cookies

Prep time: 35 minutes

Ingredients:

1 ½ cups oat flour
1 ½ cups brown rice flour
1 cup shredded Cheddar cheese
½ cup grated Parmesan cheese
1 egg
1 cup water

Instructions:

Preheat oven to 350 degrees F.

Combine all ingredients and mix together until a dough forms. Roll out onto a lightly floured surface to ¼ inch thickness. Use a cookie cutter or knife to cut into individual pieces.

Line cookie sheet with aluminum foil for easier cleanup.

Put cookies on foil-lined cookie sheet and place in oven.

Bake cookies for 20 to 25 minutes or until golden brown. Remove and allow to cool on a wire rack. Store in an airtight container in the fridge.

Recipe #63: Bacon and liver cookies

Prep time: 50 minutes

Ingredients:

1 ½ cups oat flour

1 ½ cups brown rice flour

½ lb. beef or chicken livers

6 slices bacon, cooked

1 cup oat bran

1 egg

1 cup water

Instructions:

Preheat oven to 375 degrees F. Purée livers in food processor. Grind bacon to fine bits in processor. Cleaning your food processor immediately is recommended, as the liver can harden and be hard to clean later.

Line a cookie sheet with aluminum foil for easier cleanup.

Combine all ingredients and mix together until a dough forms. Roll out onto a lightly floured surface to ¼ inch thickness. Use a cookie cutter or knife to cut into individual pieces.

Put cookies on foil-lined cookie sheet and place in oven.

Bake cookies for 22 to 27 minutes or until golden brown. Remove and allow to cool on a wire rack. Store in an airtight container in the fridge.

If you would like the cookies to be crispier, you can let them stay in the oven after you turn it off. You can remove them after a couple of hours, then store them in the refrigerator.

Recipe #64: Bacon and cheese cookies

Prep time: 35 minutes

Ingredients:

1 cup oat flour

1 cup brown rice flour

½ cup shredded Cheddar cheese

6 slices bacon, cooked

1 egg

¾ cup water

Instructions:

Preheat oven to 350 degrees F. Finely grind bacon in food processor.

Line a cookie sheet with aluminum foil for easier cleanup.

Combine all ingredients and mix together until a dough forms. Roll out onto a lightly floured surface to ¼ inch thickness. Use a cookie cutter or knife to cut into individual pieces.

Put cookies on foil-lined cookie sheet and place in oven.

Bake cookies for 20 to 25 minutes or until golden brown and the cheese begins to bubble. Remove and allow to cool on a wire rack. Store in an airtight container in the fridge.

Recipe #65: Liver and cheese cookies

Prep time: 40 minutes

Ingredients:

    1 cup oat flour

    1 ½ cups brown rice flour

    ½ lb. beef or chicken livers

    1 cup shredded Cheddar cheese

    ¼ tsp. garlic powder (optional)

    1 egg

    ½ cup water

Instructions:

Preheat oven to 350 degrees F. Purée liver in food processor. Clean processor immediately after use. Liver will cake and harden and be hard to clean off otherwise.

Line a cookie sheet with aluminum foil for easier cleanup.

Combine all ingredients and mix together until a dough forms. Roll out onto a lightly floured surface to ¼ inch thickness. Use a cookie cutter or knife to cut into individual pieces.

Put cookies on foil-lined cookie sheet and place in oven.

Bake cookies for 20 to 25 minutes or until golden brown. Remove and allow to cool on a wire rack. Store in an airtight container in the fridge.

Recipe #66: Molasses and oatmeal cookies

Prep time: 35 minutes

Ingredients:

1 ½ cups oat flour

1 ½ cups brown rice flour

½ cup old-fashioned rolled oats

¼ cup blackstrap molasses

1 egg

½ cup water

Instructions:

Preheat oven to 350 degrees F.

Line a cookie sheet with aluminum foil for easier cleanup.

Combine all ingredients and mix together until a dough forms. Roll out onto a lightly floured surface to ¼ inch thickness. Use a cookie cutter or knife to cut into individual pieces.

Put cookies on foil-lined cookie sheet and place in oven.

Bake cookies for 20 to 25 minutes or until golden brown. Remove and allow to cool on a wire rack. Store in an airtight container in the fridge.

Recipe #67: Liver and oatmeal cookies

Prep time: 40 minutes

Ingredients:

1 ½ cups oat flour

1 ½ cups brown rice flour

½ lb. beef or chicken livers

1 cup oat bran

1 ½ cup old-fashioned rolled oats

1 egg

½ cup water

Instructions:

Preheat oven to 350 degrees F. Purée liver in food processor. Clean processor immediately after use. Liver will cake and harden and be hard to clean off otherwise.

Line a cookie sheet with aluminum foil for easier cleanup.

Combine all ingredients and mix together until a dough forms. Roll out onto a lightly floured surface to ¼ inch thickness. Use a cookie cutter or knife to cut into individual pieces.

Put cookies on foil-lined cookie sheet and place in oven.

Bake cookies 25 minutes. Turn the oven off and leave the cookies on the oven rack to harden overnight. Store in an airtight container in the fridge.

Recipe #68: Doggy pâté

Prep time: 55 minutes

Ingredients:

2 cups oat flour

½ cup oat bran

1 lb. beef or chicken livers

2 eggs

1 tsp. garlic powder

Instructions:

Preheat oven to 375 degrees F. Purée liver in food processor. Clean processor immediately after use. Liver will cake and harden and be hard to clean off otherwise.

Line a 9 by 9 inch pan with aluminum foil to make cleanup easier.

Combine all of the ingredients together and mix them thoroughly. Pour liver mixture into square pan and place in oven.

Bake mixture 35 to 40 minutes or until the liver seems to be coming away from the sides of the pan.

Cool thoroughly in the pan. Slice the liver into individual portions. Store in an airtight container in the fridge.

Recipe #69: Tuna and cheese cookies

Prep time: 40 minutes

Ingredients:

1 cup oat flour
1 cup brown rice flour
½ cup oat bran
1 6-oz. can albacore tuna
½ cup shredded Cheddar cheese
1 egg
½ cup water

Instructions:

Preheat oven to 350 degrees F.

Empty contents from can of tuna, including juices, and purée in food processor.

Combine all ingredients, including puréed tuna, and mix together until a dough forms. Roll out onto a lightly floured surface to ¼ inch thickness. Use a cookie cutter or knife to cut into individual pieces.

Line cookie sheet with aluminum foil for easier cleanup.

Put tuna pieces on foil-lined cookie sheet and place in oven.

Bake cookies for 20 to 25 minutes. Remove and allow to cool on a wire rack. Store in an airtight container in the fridge.

Recipe #70: Fish treats

Prep time: 45 minutes

Ingredients:

   1 ¼ cups oat flour

   1 cup potato flour

   ½ cup oat bran

   1 cup cooked cod or other white fish

   ¼ tsp. garlic powder (optional)

   1 egg

   1 cup water

Instructions:

Preheat oven to 350 degrees F. Cook the cod or other fish and then finely grind it in the food processor.

Combine all ingredients, including the fish, and mix together until a dough forms. Roll out onto a lightly floured surface to ¼ inch thickness. Use a cookie cutter or knife to cut into individual pieces.

Line cookie sheet with aluminum foil for easier cleanup.

Put the pieces on foil-lined cookie sheet and place in oven.

Bake cookies for 20 to 25 minutes. Remove and allow to cool on a wire rack. Store in an airtight container in the fridge.

Recipe #71: Tuna training treats

Tuna is not just for cats. Lots of dogs love it. Try this quick and easy recipe that only takes 15 minutes to bake.

Prep time: 15 minutes

Ingredients:

   2 6-oz cans tuna in water, do not drain
   2 eggs
   1 to 1 ½ cup flour
   1 Tbsp. garlic powder
   Parmesan cheese

Instructions:

Mash tuna and water in a bowl with a fork to get clumps out, then liquefy in blender or food processor. Add extra drops of water if needed to liquefy completely.

Pour tuna into bowl and add flour and garlic powder; consistency should be like cake mix.

Spread tuna into greased or sprayed pan. Sprinkle with lots of Parmesan cheese. Bake at 350 degrees for 15 minutes; edges will pull away and texture will be like putty. Use a pizza cutter and slice into small squares.

Recipe #72: Cheese cookies

Most dogs love cheese. Try this easy recipe for cheese cookies.

Prep time: 15 minutes

Ingredients:

1 ½ cups whole wheat flour
1 ¼ cups grated Cheddar cheese
¼ cup margarine
milk
pinch of salt

Instructions:

Grate the cheese and let stand until it reaches room temperature.

Cream the cheese with the softened margarine, salt, and flour.

Add enough milk to the cheese mixture to form into a ball. Chill for half an hour.

Roll the cheese ball onto floured board. Cut into shapes and bake at 375 for 15 minutes or until slightly brown and firm. Makes two to three dozen, depending on size.

Recipe #73: Whole wheat cookies

You can make a great basic dog cookie in just a few minutes, and your dog will love them.

Prep time: 15 minutes

Ingredients:

2 ½ cups whole wheat flour

¼ cup wheat germ

¼ cup milk

4 Tbsp. margarine, softened

1 egg, beaten

1 Tbsp. Molasses

Instructions:

Combine flour, wheat germ, and salt in a large bowl. Cut in margarine. Stir in beaten egg, molasses, and milk. Add enough water so mixture can be shaped into a ball.

Roll dough onto a floured board to a thickness of ½ inch. Cut into shapes and place on a greased baking sheet. Bake at 375 for 15 minutes, remove from oven and let cool. Makes about 30 biscuits.

Recipe #74: Bacon biscuits

Your dog will think these bacon drop biscuits are delicious, and they are easy to make.

Prep time: 15 minutes

Ingredients:

2 eggs beaten

3 Tbsp. molasses

¼ cup vegetable oil

¼ cup milk

1 cup rolled oats

¾ cup wheat germ

¼ cup flour

¼ cup pieces of bacon

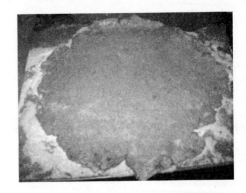

Instructions:

Mix all ingredients together and drop in teaspoons on a lightly greased sheet. Bake at 350 for 15 minutes.

Recipe #75: Homemade Frosty Paws®

Here are a couple of recipes for hot weather that your dog will love.

Prep time: 15 minutes

Ingredients:

32 oz. vanilla yogurt

1 mashed banana or one large jar of baby food

2 Tbsp. peanut butter

2 Tbsp. honey

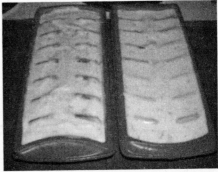

Instructions:

Blend all ingredients together and freeze in either 3-ounce paper cups or ice cube trays. Microwave just a few seconds before serving to soften.

Recipe #76: Frosty Paws (alternate version)

Prep time: 15 minutes

Ingredients:

1 ripe banana

4 oz. fat free yogurt, vanilla or banana

2 oz. water

Instructions:

Put all ingredients in blender and purée. Pour into ice cube trays or cut-down Dixie cups. Freeze.

Special Occasion Treats

Whether you want to make Halloween treats for your dog or you are planning a special "Gotcha Day!" celebration (the day you adopted your dog), there are countless special treats you can make for your dog — and some of his canine chums — to create a memorable occasion. Cookies and dog biscuits are just the beginning. If you really want to go all out for your party, you can make dog cakes and decorate them in the highest style. You can have a theme and decorate accordingly. Everything from the invitations to the party favors can be edible treats the dogs will enjoy. As long as you avoid chocolate and a few other things that are dangerous for dogs there is no reason why you and your dog could not have a ball. Most cakes and treat recipes are quite healthy, so why not pull out all the stops and celebrate?

Cakes for dogs are a wonderful way to help them celebrate special events and include them in family gatherings. You can make any occasion special and one your dog will love with these recipes.

Dog Birthday Cakes

Birthday cakes are more popular than ever right now, and these cakes are fabulous. If you check the Internet, you will find cakes that show all kinds of artistic imagination. Dog cakes today are much more than a round cake with a candle stuck on it or a sheet cake with a dog perched on top. People who love their dogs are going all out to make cakes that could rival the cakes on the Food Network. In fact, some people do get cakes for their dogs from professional bakers, but you do not need to do that to show your dog how much you love him. It is quite possible to make a gorgeous cake for your dog right at home and to decorate it in a way to make your dog and all of his doggie friends wag their tails in amazement.

So, what kind of cake do you want for your dog? Are you planning a doggie birthday party or will it be just the two of you celebrating? You can go all out or have something a little more reserved just for your dog to enjoy.

Dog Birthday Party

If you are planning to have a doggie birthday party, you will probably want a large cake. Otherwise, you can make two cakes, or you can make one cake and some cupcakes. Think of a theme for your party. Is there something that your dog particularly likes? Does he have a favorite toy? Is he good at doing something? Is he great at obedience or flyball? Does he love the park? You could take something he really loves (besides you) and use that as a theme for your cake and party.

Check pet stores and kitchen stores for small decorative items to place on your cake. And, while you are thinking about the cake, decide what shape you would like it to be. You can make the cake in any shape you like: round, square, or a dog-shaped cake. It is not that difficult to make a cake in the shape of a dog. You need to bake several round layers and then cut them into "parts" so you can attach them for the dog's head and legs and tail. Once the dog is covered in doggie cake frosting (safe for dogs), he will look like a dog. You can even make him look like your dog.

When it comes to candles, you can use Pup-Peroni® treats instead. They do not burn, but they are edible, so most dogs like them better than candles. And, you can use rawhides for invitations and send them to your dog's doggie friends. Just write the day and time of the party on the rawhides. (Hand delivery is fine.) Check your pet supply store for other things that make cute decorations and ideas for the party. Do not forget some door prizes! Use your imagination. Your dog and his friends can have some party games, too, before the cake is served.

There are some truly great dog birthday cake recipes, so choose one you think your dog will like. The icings for dog birthday cakes are especially fun because they are usually made from puréed cottage cheese or yogurt, which are both healthy for dogs. Dogs really know how to have fun and be healthy at the same time.

Here's a great birthday cake recipe for dogs:

Recipe #77: Bacon chicken layer cake

This recipe makes a real layer cake for your dog. Chicken, bacon, and yogurt will make your dog and his guests go wild.

Prep time: 75 minutes; makes ten to 12 small servings

Ingredients:

3 cups flour

1 Tbsp. baking flour

½ cup margarine, softened

6 eggs, beaten

½ cup corn oil

2 jars strained chicken baby food

2 cups finely shredded carrots

2 cups plain or vanilla yogurt

2 or 3 strips of bacon, fried crisp, then crumbled,
   or use bacon-flavored jerky strips, cut into bits

Instructions:

Generously grease and flour two 8-inch round cake pans; set aside. Combine flour and baking powder; set aside. In a mixing bowl, beat softened margarine until smooth. Add eggs and corn oil; mix well. Add strained chicken, and shredded carrots and mix until smooth. Add flour mixture and mix thoroughly. Pour batter into the two prepared 8-inch cake pans. Bake at 325 F for 60 minutes. Let cool for a few minutes before removing from pans. Cool completely on wire racks.

Place one layer on a serving plate and spread yogurt over top. Place second layer on top, then spread yogurt on top and sides of entire cake.

Sprinkle crumbled bacon or bits of jerky strips over top. Use Pup-Peroni sticks for candles.

Cakes

Most dogs seem to enjoy Halloween. They seem to like the adventure of dressing up and putting on costumes.

However, Halloween can also be a dangerous time for dogs because there is so much candy and chocolate available. Remember that chocolate is dangerous for dogs. You can provide your dog with his own chocolate substitute — carob — with this great carob cake. Have a Halloween party, either for your dog and his friends, or include your dog in your Halloween party. Just do not get the cakes mixed up, although there is nothing in this doggie cake that humans would not enjoy.

Recipe #78: Carob chip bundt cake

This is a darker, richer, peanut-flavored cake with carob chips and carob drizzled on top. This recipe makes a beautiful cake that serves 16 to 20 dogs if you are having a bigger party.

Prep time: 60 minutes; makes 20 servings

Ingredients:

1 cup whole wheat flour

1 tsp. baking soda

¼ cup peanut butter

¼ cup butter, melted

⅓ cup honey (optional)

1 egg

½ cup carob chips (carob is a chocolate substitute)*

Instructions:

Mix the dry ingredients. Add the remaining ingredients and mix quickly. Bake in a greased ring mold at 350 degrees F for 40 minutes. Drizzle melted carob over cake when cooled. Store in the refrigerator.

*Do not use chocolate chips. If you cannot find carob chips, make the cake without them.

Recipe #79: Peanut butter carrot cake

Naturally sweet, colorful, and flavorful, this cake is simple and easy to make. It is great for fall because of the colors but good anytime.

Prep time: 60 minutes; makes three to four small servings

Ingredients:

  1 cup flour
  1 tsp. baking soda
  ¼ cup peanut butter
  ¼ cup vegetable oil
  1 cup shredded carrots
  1 tsp. vanilla
  ⅓ cup honey
  1 egg

Instructions:

Mix flour and baking soda. Add remaining ingredients. Pour into greased 8-inch round cake pan and bake at 350 degrees F for 30 minutes. Let cool. Purée cottage cheese in blender for icing. Decorate with more peanut butter and carrots.

Recipe #80: Ginger banana party cake

Banana and ginger combine to make a delicious cake that is not too sweet. The aroma will fill the house. Well-chopped nuts help make it a festive cake.

Prep time: 45 minutes; makes six to eight small servings (including frosting)

Ingredients:

⅔ cup mashed bananas

½ cup softened butter

3 large eggs

¾ cup water

2 cups unbleached flour

2 tsp. baking powder

1 tsp. baking soda

1 tsp. ginger

2 tsp. cinnamon

½ cup chopped pecans

Instructions:

Beat together mashed banana and butter until creamy. Add eggs and water. Beat well. Stir in dry ingredients. Beat until smooth, Add nuts. Spoon batter evenly into oiled and floured bundt pan. Bake at 350 degrees F for about 35 minutes. Cool on wire rack five minutes, remove from pan, replace on rack and cool.

Recipe #81: Banana and mock-choc frosting

Prep time: Ten minutes;
makes 2 cups of frosting

Ingredients:

- 2 cup mashed banana
- 1 Tbsp. butter
- 6 Tbsp. powdered carob
- 2 tsp. vanilla
- 3 Tbsp. unbleached flour
- 1 tsp. cinnamon

Instructions:

Blend thoroughly and spread on cooled cake. Sprinkle with well-chopped pecans.

Decorating Tips for Treats, Cakes, and Cookies

If you go to a lot of trouble to make treats, cakes, and cookies for your dog, then you might want to do some decorating. Decorating for your dog does not have to be difficult. In fact, it can be easier than decorating baked goods for people.

Many cakes and treats for dogs can be decorated by using cottage cheese, yogurt, and cream cheese for icing. Dogs love these ingredients, and they look nice on a cake or on cookies. It is easy to use some safe food coloring if you would like a color other than white. You can also use melted carob to have a cake that looks like chocolate, and carob is perfectly fine for your dog to eat. You can buy carob in powder form or as chips at your grocery store. Mashed bananas also make a good cake topping, and dogs like them.

For decorating small cookies and cupcakes, you can use a pastry bag with a pipette. You can find them in kitchen stores and online kitchen supply sources. This allows you to use fine detail in your decorating and place swirls, flowers, or other designs just where you want them. You can even write out your dog's name if you want.

One popular idea in decorating cakes at the moment is to place a photo of you and your dog in a small frame and lay it on top of a sheet cake, then decorate around it. This kind of decoration looks nice on a cake for your dog. You can simply remove the picture and frame before serving the cake so your dog will not be tempted to eat it.

You can decorate the top of a cake with small doggie toys or with something that your dog can return to later, such as a toy or a purchased bone for dogs.

You can make your cake three-dimensional by using cardboard cutouts and standing them up in your cake. Have a dog standing up or something that means something to you and your dog. You can cover them in cream cheese or icing to make them look like part of the cake.

For Halloween cookies or Christmas treats you can take an ordinary dog cookie recipe and decorate in the colors of the season with colored doggie icing.

Remember that cinnamon and vanilla are fine to use in dog recipes. Dog cookies do not have to be bland nor do they have to be all-meat. Pumpkin is a great favorite with most dogs. So are sweet potatoes. Be willing to use some vegetables you do not ordinarily use.

You can be as creative as you want with your cookies and treats for your dog. This is one area where you can really express how you feel about your dog and what he means to you. Yes, making treats, cookies, biscuits and cakes takes some time and thought but, after all, he is your dog. He is worth it.

Cupcakes and Muffins

Cupcakes and muffins usually have a batter similar to cakes and cookies. You can use a cupcake pan or a muffin pan, depending on your preference. Small muffins in a mini loaf pan will cook quickly. Regular size muffins will take a little longer. Use cupcakes papers to line the pans. They will make cleanup easier and the cupcakes and muffins easier to handle.

Cupcakes can be decorated, or not, as you prefer. You can use plain or vanilla yogurt as an icing. Or spread a little peanut butter on top for a quick and easy topping. Muffins are not usually decorated, but it is always up to you and your dog.

Recipe #82: Blueberry muffins

Prep time: 35 minutes

Ingredients:

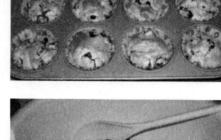

- 2 cups oat flour
- 2 tsp. baking powder
- 1 tsp. cinnamon
- 1 tsp. baking soda
- 2 cups blueberries (fresh or frozen)
- 3 eggs
- ¼ cup honey
- ¼ cup vegetable oil

Instructions:

Preheat oven to 350 degrees F.

Place cupcake papers in mini muffin pan. You can also use a regular muffin pan.

Combine all ingredients and mix thoroughly. Spoon the mixture evenly into the cupcake papers, coming close to the top of the papers.

Bake ten to 15 minutes or until a toothpick placed in the cupcake center comes back clean. Bake 20 to 25 minutes if you are using a regular muffin pan.

Remove the cupcakes or muffins from the oven and allow to cool on a wire rack. Store in an airtight container in the fridge.

Recipe #83: Peanut butter and banana cupcakes

Prep time: 30 minutes

Ingredients:

2 cups oat flour

1 tsp. baking powder

½ tsp. baking soda

¾ cup carob chips

2 eggs

1 cup bananas, mashed and puréed

1 cup peanut butter

1 tsp. vanilla

1 Tbsp. honey

¼ cup vegetable oil

Instructions:

Preheat oven to 350 degrees F. Peel bananas, mash them, and purée them in food processor.

Place cupcake papers in mini muffin pan.

Combine all ingredients and mix thoroughly. Spoon the mixture evenly in the cupcake papers, coming close to the top of the papers.

Bake ten to 15 minutes or until a toothpick placed in the cupcake center comes back cleanly.

Remove the cupcakes from the oven and allow to cool on a wire rack. Store in an airtight container in the fridge.

These cupcake can be iced with vanilla yogurt.

Recipe #84: Pumpkin muffins

Prep time: 35 minutes

Ingredients:

2 cups oat flour

2 tsp. baking flour

2 tsp. cinnamon

½ tsp. baking soda

3 eggs

¾ cup honey

¼ cup vegetable oil

1 15-oz. can pumpkin (not pie filling);
   you can also use fresh puréed pumpkin

Instructions:

Preheat oven to 350 degrees F.

Place cupcake papers in mini muffin pan. You can also use a regular muffin pan to make muffins.

Combine all ingredients and mix thoroughly. Spoon the mixture evenly into the cupcake papers, coming close to the top of the papers.

Bake ten to 15 minutes or until a toothpick placed in the cupcake center comes back cleanly. Bake 20 to 25 minutes if you are using a regular muffin pan.

Remove the cupcakes or muffins from the oven and allow to cool on a wire rack. Store in an airtight container in the fridge.

Recipe #85: Carob cupcakes

Prep time: 35 minutes

Ingredients:

1 cup oat flour

1 cup brown rice flour

2 tsp. baking soda

½ tsp. baking powder

¼ cup carob powder (do not use chocolate)

1 egg

2 Tbsp. honey

¼ cup water

¼ cup vegetable oil

½ cup plain, whole milk yogurt

Instructions:

Preheat oven to 350 degrees F.

Place cupcake papers in mini muffin pan. You can also use a regular muffin pan to make muffins.

Combine all ingredients and mix thoroughly. Spoon the mixture evenly into the cupcake papers, coming close to the top of the papers.

Bake ten to 15 minutes or until a toothpick placed in the cupcake center comes back cleanly. Bake 20 to 25 minutes if you are using a regular muffin pan.

Remove the cupcakes or muffins from the oven and allow to cool on a wire rack. Store in an airtight container in the fridge.

You can ice these cupcakes with vanilla yogurt for a yummy treat for your dog.

Recipe #86: Zucchini loaf

Prep time: 35 minutes

Ingredients:

2 cups oat flour

2 tsp. baking powder

½ tsp. baking soda

1 tsp. cinnamon

3 eggs

1 tsp. vanilla

¾ cup honey

2 cups puréed zucchini

¼ cup vegetable oil

Instructions:

Preheat oven to 325 degrees F. Purée zucchini in food processor.

Lightly grease a mini loaf pan or prepare a muffin pan with cupcake papers.

Combine all ingredients and mix thoroughly. Spoon mixture evenly into the pan, filling it close to the top.

Bake 20 to 25 minutes in either pan. The zucchini bread is done when you can insert a toothpick in the center and bring it out cleanly. Remove the loaf or cupcakes from the oven and allow them to cool completely on a wire rack. Store in an airtight container in the fridge.

Recipe #87: Banana cupcakes

Prep time: 35 minutes for cupcakes; five minutes for icing

Ingredients for cupcakes

2 cups oat flour

2 tsp. baking powder

½ tsp. baking soda

1 tsp. cinnamon

3 eggs

¼ cup honey

3 bananas, mashed and puréed

¼ cup vegetable oil

Ingredients for cupcake icing (optional)

1 cup bananas, mashed and puréed

8 oz. plain, whole milk yogurt

1 tsp. vanilla

Instructions:

Preheat oven to 350 degrees F. Peel, mash, and purée the bananas for the cupcakes in a food processor.

Line mini muffin pan with cupcake papers.

Combine all of the ingredients for the cupcakes together in a large bowl. Spoon banana mixture into cupcake papers evenly, filling them almost to the top.

Bake 12 to 15 minutes or until a toothpick inserted into the cupcake center comes out cleanly. Remove from the oven and allow to cool completely on a wire rack.

Peel, mash, and purée the bananas for the icing in a food processor. Combine icing ingredients together in a separate bowl. Decorate the cupcakes. Store in an airtight container in the fridge.

Recipe #88: Blueberry oatmeal muffins

Prep time: 45 minutes

Ingredients:

1 cup oat flour

1 cup old-fashioned rolled oats

¼ tsp. baking soda

⅔ cup honey

¼ cup vegetable oil

2 ½ cups blueberries, fresh or frozen

Instructions:

Preheat oven to 350 degrees F.

Lightly grease a muffin pan.

Combine all ingredients except for the blueberries and mix together thoroughly. Divide the mixture in half. Press half of the flour and oats mixture into the bottom of the muffin pan openings. Spread the blueberries on top of the mixture in the muffin pan. Then spread the remaining oat mixture on top of the berries.

Bake for 30 to 35 minutes or until the tops of the muffins are golden brown. Remove from the oven and allow to completely cool on a wire rack. Store in an airtight container in the fridge.

Recipe #89: Apple-cinnamon muffins

Prep time: 35 minutes

Ingredients:

- 1 ½ cups oat flour
- 1 ½ cups brown rice flour
- 1 Tbsp. baking powder
- 1 tsp. cinnamon
- 2 eggs
- ¾ cup honey
- 1 cup applesauce
- ¼ cup vegetable oil

Instructions:

Preheat oven to 350 degrees F.

Place cupcake papers in mini muffin pan. You can also use a regular muffin pan to make muffins.

Combine all ingredients and mix thoroughly. Spoon the mixture evenly into the cupcake papers coming close to the top of the papers.

Bake ten to 15 minutes or until a toothpick placed in the cupcake center comes back cleanly. Bake 20 to 25 minutes if you are using a regular muffin pan.

Remove the cupcakes or muffins from the oven and allow to cool on a wire rack. Store in an airtight container in the fridge.

Recipe #90: Apple and carrot muffins

Prep time: 30 minutes for the muffins; you can make the muffins various sizes

Prep time: Ten minutes for the frosting, more for decorating

Ingredients:

Muffins:

2 cups shredded carrots

3 eggs

½ cup applesauce, unsweetened

2 tsp. cinnamon

½ cup rolled oats

3 cups whole wheat flour

Frosting:

8 oz. low-fat cream cheese, softened

¼ cup applesauce, unsweetened

Instructions for muffins:

Preheat oven to 350 F.

Lightly spray cups of muffin tin.

In a large bowl, stir together the carrots, eggs, and applesauce. Set aside.

In another medium bowl, whisk together the cinnamon, oats, and flour.

Slowly mix in the dry ingredients. Stir until well blended.

Spoon mixture into muffin tin. The dough will be thick, so you may wet your fingers to press the dough into place.

The dog cupcake will not rise much, so do not worry about overfilling the muffin tin.

Bake for 25 minutes.

Cool completely on a wire rack before frosting or serving.

Instructions for frosting:

Blend both ingredients with a hand mixer until well blended.

Spoon into a pastry bag for easy decorating.

Storing:

These dog cupcakes will keep fresh in your refrigerator for two weeks. You can freeze them for up to two months. If you are going to freeze them, do not decorate with the frosting until they have thawed.

The Best Ingredients for Dog Treats

If you examine many dog treat recipes, it probably will not take you long to reach the conclusion that they are not that different from the recipes used to make cookies for people. The basic ingredients of dog cookies and cookies for people are often the same: flour, eggs, milk, butter. You can usually tell it is a dog treat recipe when you read "purée liver" or "½ cup bacon bits," although there may be some hors d'oeuvres for people with similar ingredients.

The quality of your treats and cookies for your dog will depend a great deal on the quality of the ingredients you use. There are some things you can do to ensure that your dog biscuits and cookies are as healthy as possible. Here are a few tips:

1. Always look over a recipe to make sure all of the ingredients are safe for dogs. Chocolate is always a no-go. Use carob as a substitute. Raisins, grapes, and macadamia nuts can be toxic to dogs. Leave them out of recipes. Onion in small amounts probably will not hurt your dog, but large amounts might result in anemia-related toxicity, so you might want to remove onions from recipes.

2. If your dog requires a special diet or if he has allergies, always make sure any cookies or treats you make for him (or purchase) also meet his dietary needs. For instance, if your dog is allergic to wheat, you need to be careful about cookies and treats, as many of them are made with wheat flour. If you plan to make treats for your dog, use a different kind of flour — one that your dog can tolerate. You can also look for grain-free recipes. Always read the labels on cookies and treats before you buy them to see what the ingredients are if you have a dog with allergies.

3. If your dog has kidney or liver problems, look for recipes that are low in fat, phosphorus, and protein.

4. Go easy on sweets in any recipe for your dog. Remember that refined sugar is not any better for your dog than it is for you. If the recipe calls for a sugar source, try to use molasses or honey instead of sugar.

5. There are many low-cal and natural ingredients available these days. Try some of them when you are making your dog's treats, especially if you are helping your dog watch his weight. When recipes call for cottage cheese, use low-cal and fat-free versions. Remember that some 40 percent of dogs in the U.S. are estimated to be overweight or obese. Your dog does not have to be one of them. You can also look for ingredients that are lower in sodium.

6. Baby food often makes a good substitute for some of the puréed meats called for in some dog treat recipes. A jar of beef baby food is a good substitute for puréed liver, for example, unless you really want to make your dog happy with liver. The baby food is easy to find and easy to handle in the kitchen, and there is far less mess than when you purée meats. However, you still need to use liver and other organ meats and not baby food when making your dog's meals.

Remember that when you do give your dog treats or feed him cake for dogs, it is not necessary to let him stuff himself. A few treats are plenty. A few bites of cake are enough. Treats, cookies, biscuits, and cake are extras. Do not let your dog make himself obese on treats.

Recipe #91: Low protein/low fat/ low phosphorus cookies

For dogs with kidney disease, pancreatitis, or liver problems you can try the following cookie recipe because it is low in fat, protein, and phosphorus.

Prep time: 30 minutes; makes four 1-cup servings

Ingredients:

2 ½ cups rice flour or white all-purpose bleached flour (these two are lowest in phosphorus, which is best for kidney disease)

½ tsp. garlic powder

6 Tbsp. low sodium, low-fat chicken broth*

½ cup cold water

1 cup cooked vegetables ground up (zucchini and sweet potatoes are low in phosphorus, which is best for kidney disease)

Instructions:

Combine flour and garlic.

Add chicken broth and vegetable(s) to flour.

Add enough cold water to the flour and broth mix to form a ball; pat dough to ½ inch thick and cut into desired shapes; place on non-stick cookie sheet and bake in preheated oven at 350 degrees F for 25 minutes. Cool on a wire rack. Freeze what is not eaten within a week.

See Chapter 6 for the low-fat chicken broth recipe.

Favorite Treat Recipes

There are, without doubt, thousands or hundreds of thousands of dog treat recipes online. Some of them are variations of a few basic recipes (there are probably hundreds of recipes for liver treats), but there are also many different recipes. Here are some that we have tried and that our dogs have loved.

Recipe #92: Liver bread

Prep time: 30 minutes; makes as many pieces as you would like

Ingredients:

   1 lb. of any kind of liver, puréed
   1 cup of flour
   1 cup of corn meal
   2 Tbsp. of garlic powder
   1 Tbsp. of oil

Instructions:

Purée the liver and mix in the other ingredients. Spread on a cookie sheet or jellyroll pan. Bake at 350 degrees F for about 25 minutes. Cool and break in pieces.

Recipe #93: Liver brownies (and variations)

Prep time: 30 minutes

Ingredients:

1 lb. liver, any kind

1 cup corn meal

1 ½ cups flour

1 tsp. fresh minced garlic or ½
    tsp garlic powder

1 tsp. fennel or anise seed

½ tsp. salt

Instructions:

Pat liver dry with paper towel. Cut into small chunks and grind in blender or food processor.

In large bowl, mix liver with corn meal and flour. This will be stiff, and the flour might not all blend in. Gradually add garlic and salt.

Spread mixture on greased cookie sheet.

Bake at 350 degrees F for 20 minutes. Allow to cool ten minutes; cut into squares. May be refrigerated or frozen.

Tips:

You can change this recipe around by changing the ingredients.

You can also add:

A whole egg or two

Fresh yogurt

Grated raw carrots or apples

Crushed walnuts

Coriander, caraway, etc.

Use your imagination.

Recipe #94: Homemade Natural Balance® meat roll

Rollover and Natural Balance meat rolls are popular with dogs. You can make your own version at home.

Prep time: 45 minutes

Ingredients:

1 lb. organ meat, such as liver

Garlic

Assorted spices

1 package Jiffy corn muffin mix

Instructions:

Grind up 1 pound of organ meat, any flavor, in a blender or food processor. Add raw garlic and spices to your heart's content. Put in one package of Jiffy corn muffin mix. Pour into a baking pan to a depth of ¼ to ½ inch. Bake at 375 degrees F until just the middle of the meat is still red, then turn off the oven and let the center cook. Slice it up and put it in baggies for your fridge.

There is almost no end to the things you can do to liver: boil it, microwave it, freeze it and cut it, bake it. Go in your kitchen and play with some liver. Your dogs will love whatever you do.

Recipe #95: Turkey treats

Prep time: 45 minutes

Ingredients:

    1 lb. ground turkey (not turkey sausage)

    1 cup oatmeal

    1 egg

    Parmesan cheese

    Garlic powder

Instructions:

Mix all ingredients together using hands and pat into a greased loaf pan.

Bake at 350 degrees F for 30 to 35 minutes. Cool thoroughly, then cut into thick strips (these treats do not hold together when slicing into small squares).

Freeze unused portions and keep the portions you are using refrigerated. The finished treats will have the consistency of meatloaf.

Recipe #96: Salmon cookies

Prep time: 40 minutes

Ingredients:

    15 oz. can of salmon or Jack mackerel

    Flour

    2 tsp. salt

    1 tsp. baking powder

    Garlic powder (optional)

Instructions:

Mix together fish, plus all liquid from can, salt, baking powder, and add enough flour for texture.

Spread fish mixture out on cookie sheet. Score into sections so the cookies will be easier to break apart when done.

Bake at 350 degrees F for about 30 minutes or until crust is golden.

Store in container in fridge or freezer for longer periods of time.

Recipe #97: Peanut butter treats

Prep time: 30 minutes

Ingredients:

2 Tbsp. corn oil

½ cup peanut butter

1 cup water

1 cup whole wheat flour

2 cups white flour

Instructions:

Preheat oven to 350 degrees F.

Combine oil, peanut butter, and water. Add flour to the peanut butter mixture 1 cup at a time, then knead into firm dough.

Roll dough to ¼ inch thickness and cut with small bone-shaped cookie cutter.

Bake at 350 degrees F for 20 minutes. Makes two and a half dozen.

Recipe #98: Turkey sausages

Prep time: 20 minutes

Ingredients:

Ground turkey meat (any amount)

Low sodium breadcrumbs

Parmesan cheese

Parsley flakes

Instructions:

In a large mixing bowl, add 1 teaspoon of parsley per pound of meat and 1 tablespoon of Parmesan cheese per pound of meat.

Stir in breadcrumbs until the mixture is somewhat dry. You should be able to form small balls and roll sausage-shaped treats between your hands without having the mixture stick to your hands (too moist) or crumble apart (too dry).

Place on jelly roll pan lined with aluminum foil.

Bake at 350 degrees F until the sausages are lightly browned on the outside and fully cooked on the inside.

Place the sausages on absorbent paper towels and blot to remove excess grease.

Store cooled sausages in zip-close bags in the freezer.

For training treats, cut sausages into raisin-sized pieces.

Recipe #99: Peanut butter biscuits

Prep time: 45 minutes

Ingredients:

4 cups whole wheat flour

2 cups oatmeal

½ to ¾ cup chunky peanut butter

2 ½ cups hot water

Instructions:

Mix all ingredients, adding more hot water if dough is too sticky. Knead well.

Roll out dough to ¼ inch thickness and cut into shapes with cookie cutter.

Bake on greased cookie sheet at 350 degrees F for 40 minutes.

Turn off heat and let cool in oven overnight.

Great Training Treats

Lots of people make treats and cookies for their dogs just for fun. They like having a snack to give their dogs around the house. But many people make treats for their dogs because they train them either at home or go to classes with them. Positive reinforcement and clicker training, in particular, make great use of rewards for dogs, and this often means being able to give your dog tiny treats again and again during a training session. In the case of clicker training, you want the treat to be something that your dog loves. But it also has to be small, so your dog will not fill up on it quickly. You might have to repeat a lesson again and again when you are trying to teach your dog something.

Here are some suggestions for treats that work well for training:

Recipe #100: Liver bait

Prep time: 30 minutes

Ingredients:

1 lb. of finely ground raw liver

1 cup flour

½ cup cornmeal

1 to 3 Tbsp. garlic salt

Instructions:

Mix all of the ingredients together.

Spread on a lightly greased piece of tin foil on a cookie sheet. This mixture is thick — like wet cement.

Bake at 350 degrees F for 30 minutes.

When the liver is done, peel off the tin foil, break the liver into pieces, and then freeze in packages to fit your needs.

Tips:

This bait will keep without refrigeration for at least a week if it is not in the sun or extreme heat. It breaks into small pieces easily. It will keep for several weeks in the refrigerator; it can be frozen and refrozen numerous times, and it thaws in less than five minutes. And dogs love it. Freeze unused portions in sealed bags.

Optional ingredients you can use include eggs, cottage cheese, grated Cheddar or Parmesan cheese, oatmeal, other grains, grated carrots or apples, or several cloves of garlic run through the grinder in place of the garlic salt.

Recipe #101: Ma Barker biscuits

Prep time: 20 minutes

Ingredients:

2 eggs beaten

3 Tbsp. molasses

¼ cup vegetable oil

¼ cup milk

1 cup rolled oats

¾ cup wheat germ

¼ cup flour

¼ cup bacon bits (optional)

Instructions:

Mix all of the ingredients together and drop by teaspoons on a lightly greased sheet. Bake at 350 degrees F for 15 minutes.

Do not forget the always popular hotdog bits. You can slice a hotdog wiener into small bits, and most dogs love them. Or you can use Vienna sausages. Some people prefer to pop the hotdog bits into the microwave for a few seconds. Popcorn also makes a great training treat, and it is low calorie.

Many dog show handlers swear by baked chicken. You can jazz it up various ways, but with the basic method, you salt the chicken (no skin or bones) with garlic salt and place on a cooking sheet in the oven on low heat (200 F) for a couple of hours. Let it cook until it is partly dried out. Then slice into small, bait-size pieces. Dogs go wild. Handlers say it tastes good, too, as they often have to put the bait in their mouths when they are in the show ring. Most handlers prefer it to liver.

Chapter 9

Storage and Travel

n this chapter, we will discuss some important food safety guidelines. Making food for your dog has some things in common with making food for yourself and your family. Fortunately, dogs are not as susceptible to problems with E. coli and salmonella as humans are, but when you handle food for your dog, you are still susceptible to these organisms and you need to take care.

Food Safety Guidelines

The USDA publishes an excellent 27-page PDF document titled Kitchen Companion: Your Safe Food Handbook. It is too long to reproduce here, but this handbook is highly recommended for anyone who cooks at home for their dog. You can download it online at **www.fsis.usda.gov/PDF/Kitchen_Companion.pdf**.

If you follow good kitchen hygiene practices, you will avoid problems with most bacteria and viruses, especially the ones that could be spread to humans. Keep the following safety rules in mind:

- Wash your hands between each task you do in the kitchen.

- Avoid cross-contamination. Use a different cutting board and utensils for raw foods and cooked foods, as well as different cutting boards and utensils for raw meats and vegetables.

- Always use clean dishes and bowls, even for your dog's food.

- Serve hot foods hot and cold foods cold. Hot foods should be above 140 degrees F. Cold foods should be below 40 degrees F.

- Food should not be left at room temperature for more than two hours.

- Thaw foods in the refrigerator, not at room temperature.

- Do not allow meats to drip on other food when they thaw.

- If you are storing hot food, refrigerate it right away in a shallow container so it will cool faster.

- Store food as soon as you are finished with it. Throw away any food that you are not sure about. If in doubt, throw it out. Do not eat something or feed it to your dog if you have doubts about its freshness or whether it is spoiled.

Dogs are susceptible to E. coli, salmonella, and other bacteria, but the greatest danger from these organisms is to you, so be careful when handling raw meats and other foods in the kitchen.

Storage, Serving, and Heating Suggestions

When it comes to serving homemade food to your dog, you can basically follow the same rules that you would follow for serving meals to your family. The food is much the same, made from similar ingredients. It follows recipes that are similar to human meals. If the food has been stored in the refrigerator, warm it for your dog. You can warm it in a pot on your stovetop or heat it up in the microwave for a minute or two.

If you store the food in individual plastic bags that seal or which you can tie, you only need to bring out an individual portion to warm up for your dog. You can also store the food in Tupperware-type tubs if you plan to store several servings together. Be sure to label your plastic bags and Tupperware-type tubs with the kind of meal, date, and other important information so it will be easy to identify the food.

If you bake lots of cookies and treats for your dog, you probably do not want to give them all to him in just a day or two. Cookies, cupcakes, and other treats in this book freeze well, and they are easy to thaw. You can put them in plastic bags or plastic tubs according to how many you want to take out for your dog at one time.

Most of the recipes given in this book will last up to a week in the refrigerator if they are kept in individual plastic bags or in a Tupperware-type tub. You can freeze them in your freezer for up to six months before they will get some freezer burn. Remember that the longer the food is frozen, the more the nutrients will start to disappear from the food. The fresher the food, the more nutritious it is.

Feeding Your Dog While Traveling

Feeding your dog while traveling can pose problems for owners who cook for their dogs. If you go on vacation with your dog, for example, you might not have access to a kitchen or feel like spending a lot of time in a kitchen preparing food for your dog's dinner. Some owners solve this problem by temporarily switching their dogs to an acceptable kibble while they are away from home or feeding canned food. However, other owners find ways to continue feeding their dog a homemade diet.

If you would like to go on feeding your dog his regular homecooked meals while the two of you are away from home, you can prepare his meals in advance, freeze them, and store them in an ice-filled cooler while you travel. Once you reach a motel or hotel with your dog, you can place them in a small refrigerator in the room. Use a small microwave in the room to heat the meals. This method largely depends on you traveling by car with your dog because you will need to keep the meals on ice while you are in transit.

Some larger cities, such as New York and San Francisco, also have butcher shops that sell pre-made meals for owners who want to feed homemade meals to their dogs but who do not have the time (or the facilities) to cook. If you are traveling to another city with your dog, you can check and see in advance if there are any butcher shops that offer this service. Some gourmet pet stores might also offer homecooked meals to go.

Still, the safest bet is usually to take your own homemade food for your dog if possible. Then you will know what is in the food and how it was made. It is the food that your dog is used to eating.

If your dog will be staying with friends or if he is being boarded, make his food in advance, freeze it, and take it with him so the people caring for him can feed him. They will only need to thaw it (in the refrigerator) and heat it up.

Chapter 10

Wrap-Up

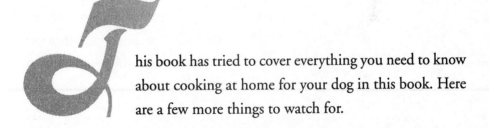

his book has tried to cover everything you need to know about cooking at home for your dog in this book. Here are a few more things to watch for.

Is Homemade Working for Your Dog?

Most dogs do well on a homemade diet, but how will you know if your dog is doing well? The best way is by looking at him. Is he losing weight? Is he gaining too much weight? What does his coat look like? Does he have healthy-looking skin? Are his eyes bright and alert? Does he have clean, white-pink ears that smell good? These are all important ways to tell if your dog is healthy.

If your dog is not doing well on a homecooked diet, you can do several things. You can use different recipes to make sure he is getting all of the nutrients he needs in his diet. Be sure he is getting the calcium he needs as well as a good multivitamin each day. He might need a green blend, too, or some other supplements. He might do better on a different diet. For example, he might do better on a good commercial diet. Although they are often maligned today, dogs have been eating commercial diets for

about 100 years, and many dogs have lived long, healthy lives on them. The best commercial foods have some good meat protein sources. So, if your dog does not do well on a homemade diet, it is not the end of the world. Keep trying different things to find the right food for him.

You can also talk to your vet if your dog has any specific skin or health problems or signs of allergies, or make an appointment with a canine nutritionist.

What If You Cannot Cook for Your Dog All the Time?

If you cannot cook for your dog all the time but you are concerned about his nutrition, do not feel bad. You obviously care about your dog and you are trying to feed him a healthy diet. You might wish to combine some elements of a commercial diet with a homemade diet. Feed your dog a good kibble and add some homemade food to it. You can add up to about 25 to 30 percent homemade food to your dog's diet without dangerously altering the nutritional balance of a commercial food. If you add more homemade food than that, you risk your dog getting too much or too little of the vitamins, minerals, and other nutrients he needs in his diet.

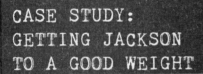

CASE STUDY:
GETTING JACKSON
TO A GOOD WEIGHT

Mari Anderson

Mari Anderson has been cooking to supplement her dogs' main diet for about 18 months.

I have always added fruits and vegetables to my dogs' diets, but I started cooking specifically for my dog Jackson when I needed to change his diet. Jackson was burning through his chicken-based kibble, eating four cups of kibble per day, yet he weighed only 54 pounds. He is an average-sized English Setter male and was very skinny at that weight. He also has persistent urinary crystals, and his pH has been off.

My vet wanted me to get him off chicken or lamb as his primary source of protein and to add water-containing foods for the urinary problems. He is not allergic to anything, but my vet said chicken and lamb are "too hot" for him. She wanted him off all kibble and would like me to cook all his meals using a specific balanced diet. However, I don't have the inclination or storage space to prepare completely homecooked meals. I did go out and buy a set of cookware, and I make the doggy stew to provide good nutrition and minimize the amount of kibble Jackson gets.

I don't follow a specific diet. My vet gave me a verbal list of foods I should add to Jackson's diet, and this is the basis for the "doggy stew," as I call it. I also add some of the foods raw in small amounts, and I have been doing that for several years.

This doggy stew is usually based on brown rice and sweet potatoes, but if I am in a hurry, I use couscous or quinoa, which cook very quickly, instead of the rice, and microwave those with some vegetables. To the base, I add whatever fruits and vegetables that are in my refrigerator and on my counters. Jackson is supposed to have foods with high water content, so usual ingredients will be summer squash, cut up apples, pears or peaches, lettuce, cucumbers, and mushrooms. I've added blueberries, regular potatoes, carrots, etc.

I feed my two girls a good kibble (Kirkland chicken and vegetable kibble) as their main diet. I feed Jackson Honest Kitchen Keen, which is turkey based, as his main food. I also give him a small amount of CostCo turkey and sweet potato kibble and supplement with the doggy stew. On evenings when I give him a substantial amount of the stew, I don't give him the kibble. I add plain yogurt to each one's dinner and small amounts of fruits and vegetables as I cut them up for my own meals. They also all get supplements such as glucosamin and fish oil.

I also add extra protein, especially to Jackson. I give the girls each a chicken "wingette" (bought in 4- to 5-pound bags frozen at the regular grocery store) every couple of days. These have the bone in to provide chewing activity and help keep their teeth clean. As Jackson is supposed to avoid chicken, I give him cut up pieces of turkey necks or wings, beef chuck bones or pork neck bones. I feed them raw but defrosted. Jackson is supposed to have organ meats, fish, eggs, etc., so I try to give him those things on days when he doesn't get the bones. I give the same things to my girls but sometimes in lesser amounts. Some days, I add canned food instead. I have been buying Evanger's canned beef or duck. But some days, they don't get any food supplements at all. Ours is a casual household.

The Honest Kitchen is not cheap, but with some kibble and the doggy stew, I feed about a 10-pound box of it each month to Jackson. Jackson has gained seven or eight pounds (went from 54 pounds to an average of 60 to 62 pounds, which is a good weight for him). He still has crystals in his urine, but on his last urinalysis, they were much lessened. He also still has trouble with his pH. His coat looks and feels good, as do those of my other dogs. People, including some of my ES (English Setter) friends, always are commenting on how good my dogs' coats feel.

I estimate it takes about 20 minutes to half an hour to prepare their meals. However, cooking the doggy stew takes longer. It can take 20 minutes to half an hour to cut up the ingredients, then usually cooks for close to an hour (I use brown rice and sweet potatoes as the base, so has to cook until those are done). I usually cook up enough for four to five days, then just reheat some of it each night. Then I may go another three or even four nights with no doggy stew, until I make up another big batch.

I would definitely recommend homecooking to others, especially if they have a dietary challenged dog. My other dogs also like the homecooked supplement, as well as the bits and pieces of the fruits and vegetables I fix for myself.

I like my method of cooking only to supplement a commercial diet and minimize kibble for Jackson. This way, I know my dogs are getting a balanced diet using the commercial food as a base, yet I am providing extra nutrition. Furthermore, I feel good knowing I am giving my dogs something special, and they love the extra food.

Conclusion

For those of you who do cook for your dog, try to remember that it should be fun. So often people who cook for their dog worry constantly about their dog's diet. They analyze dog poop and become stressed about the nutritional content of every ingredient in their dog's food. That can lead to dogs that are stressed, too.

Cooking for your dog can be something that you do for your dog out of love. It can be something that you do with your kids to teach them about caring for pets. It can be a fun activity for the entire family. Cooking for your dog does not have to be any more difficult than cooking for your family. You can keep your dog happy and healthy without driving yourself crazy.

Although it is not a good idea to let children play with knives or other sharp utensils, there are lots of recipes here that call for stirring and mixing. You can put your children to work when it comes to mixing things in bowls, rolling out dough for cookies, helping with cutting out cookies, and feeding cookies and treats to the dogs. They will get lots of kudos from your dog when it comes to the final product.

We hope **Canine Cuisine: 101 Natural Dog Food & Treat Recipes to Make Your Dog Healthy and Happy** has been helpful to you and that it has provided you with lots of tasty recipes that your dog will love. The recipes provided here are not only homemade, they are also healthy for your dog. You can find most of the ingredients right on your grocery store shelves, if you do not already have them in your kitchen. If you follow these recipes, you will be showing your dog how much you love him, and that will make your dog one happy pooch.

Nutritional Guidelines

DAILY RECOMMENDED ALLOWANCES FOR PROTEIN AND FATS

	PUPPIES (WEIGHING 12 LBS, 33 LBS AT MATURITY)	ADULT DOGS (WEIGHING 33 LBS)	PREGNANT/ NURSING DOGS (WEIGHING 33 LBS WITH SIX PUPPIES
Crude* Protein	56 g	25 g	69 g/158 g
Total Fat	21 g	14 g	29 g/67 g

*"Crude" refers to the specific method of testing the product, not to the quality of the nutrient itself. Crude protein is the amount of protein in a food based simply on the approximate nitrogen measurement.

Table from the pamphlet *Nutrient Requirements of Dogs and Cats*, from the National Academies Press, 2006.

Weights are given in grams. If you have a kitchen scale then you should be able to weigh your ingredients in grams without any problem.

AVERAGE DAILY ENERGY NEEDS
CALORIES PER DAY
(Kilocalories per day*)

TYPE OF DOG	10 LBS	30 LBS	50 LBS	70 LBS	90 LBS
PUPPIES (10 lb puppy growing to 33 lbs at maturity)	990				
INACTIVE DOGS (dogs with little stimulus or opportunity to exercise)	296	674	989	1272	1540
ADULT ACTIVE DOGS (dogs with strong stimulus and ample opportunity to exercise, such as dogs in households with more than one dog, in the country or with a yard)	404	922	1353	1740	2100
PREGNANT DOGS (from 4 weeks after mating until delivery)	518	1274	1340	2570	3170
YOUNG ADULT ACTIVE DOGS	446	993	1451	1876	2264
OLDER ACTIVE DOGS	327	745	1093	1407	1700

*1 Calorie = 1 kilocalorie = 1,000 calories. The term Calorie that is used on food nutrition labels is really a "food calorie," sometimes called a "large calorie." It is equivalent to 1,000 calories (or 1 kilocalorie) as calories are defined scientifically (the amount of energy needed to warm 1 gram of water at 1 degree C). In *Nutrient Requirements of Dogs and Cats*, energy needs are expressed in terms of kilocalories, which are equivalent to Calories in this document.

Table from the pamphlet *Nutrient Requirements of Dogs and Cats*, from the National Academies Press, 2006.

The calories given here are suggestions for dogs of various weights and activity levels. Your dog might have different needs. These calorie suggestions should only be used as a starting point. You can reduce or increase calories for your dog as needed based on your dog's condition. Your dog may need more or fewer calories at different times of the year, for example. If you have a dog that is sexually intact, then your dog may have different caloric needs at different times in her estrus cycle. Always pay attention to your dog's weight and condition, and use your best judgment about how much to feed.

VITAMINS NEEDED BY DOGS

VITAMIN	WHAT IT DOES	DAILY NEEDS	DEFICIENCY RESULTS IN
Vitamin K	Activation of clotting factors, bone proteins, and other proteins	0.41 mg	No reports of naturally occurring deficiencies in normal dogs
Vitamin B1 (Thiamin)	Energy and carbohydrate metabolism; activation of ion channels in neural tissue	0.56 mg	Failure to grow, weight loss and neurological abnormalities in puppies; damage to the nervous system and to the heart in adult dogs
Riboflavin	Enzyme functions	1.3 mg	Anorexia; weight loss; muscular weakness; flaking dermatitis; eye lesions
Vitamin B6	Glucose generation; red blood cell function; niacin synthesis; nervous system function; immune response; hormone regulation; gene activation.	0.4 mg	Anorexia and weight loss in puppies; convulsions, muscle twitching, and anemia in adult dogs Impairment of motor control and balance; muscle weakness.
Niacin	Enzyme functions	4 mg	Anorexia; weight loss; inflammation of the lips, cheeks, and throat; profuse salivation; bloody diarrhea; bloody feces; convulsions
Pantothenic Acid	Energy metabolism	4 mg	Erratic food intake; sudden prostration or coma; rapid respiratory and heart rates; convulsions; gastrointestinal symptoms; reduced antibody production
Vitamin B12	Enzyme functions	9µg	Appetite loss; lack of white blood cells; anemia; bone marrow changes
Folic Acid	Amino acid and nucleotide metabolism; mitochondrial protein synthesis.	68µg	Weight loss; decline in hemoglobin concentration
Choline	Phospholipid cell membrane component	425 mg	Loss of body weight; fatty liver

*Daily needs for an adult dog weighing 33 pounds, consuming 1,000 Calories per day. g = grams; mg = milligrams; µg = micrograms

Table from the pamphlet *Nutrient Requirements of Dogs and Cats,* **from the National Academies Press, 2006.**

DAILY RECOMMENDED ALLOWANCES FOR MINERALS

MINERALS	FUNCTIONS	DAILY RECOMMENDED ALLOWANCES*	SIGNS OF DEFICIENCIES/ EXCESS
Calcium	Formation of bones and teeth; blood coagulation nerve impulse transmission; muscle contraction; cell signaling	0.75 g	Nutritional secondary hyperparathyroidism; significant decreases in bone mineral content, which can result in major skeletal abnormalities, especially in growing puppies of large breeds
Phosphorus	Skeletal structure; DNA and RNA structure; energy metabolism; locomotion; acid-base balance	0.75 g	Reduced weight gain; poor appetite; bowing and swelling of forelimbs in puppies
Magnesium	Enzyme functions; muscle and nerve-cell membrane stability; hormone secretion and function; mineral structure of bones and teeth	150 mg	Reduction in weight gain, irritability, and convulsions in puppies; hyperextension of carpal joints and hind-leg paralysis later in life
Sodium	Acid-base balance; regulation of osmotic pressure; nerve impulse generation and transmission	100 mg	Restlessness; increased heart rate, water intake, and hemoglobin concentration; dry and tacky mucus membranes
Potassium	Acid-base balance; nerve-impulse transmission; enzymatic reactions; transport functions impulse transmission; enzymatic	1 g	Poor growth in puppies; paralysis of neck muscles and rear legs; general weakness later in life
Chlorine	Acid-base balance; transfer of extracellular fluids across cell membranes	150 mg	Reduced weight gain and weakness in puppies

Iron	Synthesis of blood components; energy metabolism	7.5 mg	Poor growth; pale mucous membranes; lethargy; weakness; diarrhea. At acute levels, dangerous oxidative reactions that lead to gastrointestinal and other tissue damage
Copper	Connective tissue formation; iron metabolism; blood cell formation melanin pigment formation; myelin formation; defense against oxidative damage	1.5 mg	Loss of hair pigmentation in puppies; anemia
Zinc	Enzyme reactions; cell replication; protein and carbohydrate metabolism; skin function; wound healing	15 mg	Poor weight gain; vomiting; skin lesions
Manganese	Enzyme functions; bone development; neurological function	1.2 mg	No studies of deficiency in dogs
Selenium	Defense against oxidative damage; immune response	90 µg	Anorexia; depression; breathing discomfort; coma; muscular degeneration
Iodine	Thyroid hormone synthesis; cell differentiation; growth and development of puppies; regulation of metabolic rate	220 µg	Enlargement of thyroid glands; dry, sparse hair coat; weight gain; excessive tearing, salivation, and nasal discharge; dandruff

*Daily needs for an adult dog weighing 33 pounds, consuming 1,000 Calories per day.

g = grams; mg = milligrams; µg = micrograms

Table from the pamphlet *Nutrient Requirements of Dogs and Cats*, from the National Academies Press, 2006.

DAILY RECOMMENDED ALLOWANCES FOR VITAMINS

VITAMIN	FUNCTIONS	DAILY RECOMMENDED ALLOWANCES*	SIGNS OF DEFICIENCIES/ EXCESS
Vitamin A	Vision; growth; immune function; fetal development; cellular differentiation; transmembrane protein transfer	379µg	Anorexia; body weight loss; ataxia; conjunctivitis; corneal disorders; skin lesions; respiratory ailments; increased susceptibility to infection. Imbalance in bone remodeling processes; artery and vein degeneration; dehydration; central nervous system depression; joint pain
Vitamin D	Maintenance of mineral status; phosphorus balance	3.4µg	Rickets; lethargy; loss of muscle tone; bone swelling and bending Anorexia; weakness; diarrhea; vomiting; calcification of soft tissue; excessive mineralization of long bones; dehydration; dry and brittle hair; muscle atrophy
Vitamin E	Defense against oxidative damage	8 mg	Degeneration of skeletal muscle; reproductive failure; retinal degeneration

Table from the pamphlet *Nutrient Requirements of Dogs and Cats*, from the National Academies Press, 2006.

Additional Resources

Anne, Jonna, Mary Straus, Shawn Messonnier. *The Healthy Dog Cookbook: 50 Nutritious & Delicious Recipes Your Dog Will Love.* Neptune City, NJ: T.F.H. Publications, 2008.

This book offers 50 nutritious recipes for your dog. There are menus for every size and type of dog, including dogs that have allergies and other problems. The book includes recipes for meals as well as snacks and treats. The recipes are generally easy and inexpensive. Recipes include a nutrition panel and a portion calculator. Written with the help of a canine nutritionist and consulting vet.

Billinghurst, Ian. *Barf Diet: For Cats and Dogs.* Australia: Ian Gregory Billinghurst, 2001.

This may not be the be-all, end-all of books on the raw diet for dogs, but it is essential to your library if you are thinking of feeding your dogs raw. Dr. Billinghurst covers everything. People who feed a raw diet to their dogs have been using this book for years to help them feed their dogs a healthy diet, along with *Give Your Dog A Bone*, also by Dr. Billinghurst.

Moore, Arden. *Real Food for Dogs: 50 Vet-Approved Recipes to Please the Canine Gastronome*. North Adams, MA: Storey, 2009.

This recipe book contains many recipes approved by a vet that will satisfy your dog's every craving. Also, you will be delighted by Anne Davis' fun illustrations that highlight recipes and make the book interesting for the chef in all of us.

Pitcairn, Richard H., DVM, and Susan Hubble Pitcairn. *Dr. Pitcairn's New Complete Guide to Natural Health for Dogs and Cats*. Emmaus, PA: Rodale Press, 2005.

Considered a classic. This book was written by two veterinary specialists in chemical-free nutrition, treatment, and natural healing for pets. The book actually covers much more than just nutrition, including the dog's environment, exercise, and caring for a sick animal. This is a holistic approach to pet care.

Quadrillion Press, Dan Dye, Mark Beckloff. *Three Dog Bakery Cookbook: Over 50 Recipes for All-Natural Treats for Your Dog.* Riverside, NJ: Andrews McMeel, 1998.
The top-selling pet cookbook on Amazon.com. The Three Dog Bakery is famous for its cookies and treats, and your pet will probably love them, too. Not a complete cookbook, but the treat recipes are excellent.

Rees, Wendy Nan, and Kevin Schlanger, *The Natural Pet Food Cookbook: Healthful Recipes for Dogs and Cats.* Howell, 2007.
Written after the pet food recalls of 2007, the book provides 50 vet-approved, pet-tested recipes ranging from basic kibble to casseroles and stews. It discusses cooking techniques, food selection, and more. It provides information on storing and freezing homemade pet foods. The author also gives information about the nutritional requirements of cats and dogs and discusses potentially harmful foods.

Roberts, Donna Twitchell. *Good Food Cookbook for Dogs.* Beverley, MA: Quarry Books, 2004.
The book provides more than 50 recipes for stews, casseroles, snacks, and treats for your dog. It also gives information on feeding dogs that have special health problems. It is said to be a sensible and wholesome approach to cooking for dogs.

Strombeck, Donald R. *Home-Prepared Dog & Cat Diets: the Healthful Alternative.* Wiley-Blackwell, 1999.

Offers over 200 computer-balanced recipes. Contains nutrient content data for each recipe, including proteins, fats, and calories. Gives nutritional guidance and describes special diets for pets who need them. Offers recipe categories to manage obesity and diseases that affect the gastrointestinal system, skin, kidneys, and the pancreas.

Bibliography

Fox, Michael, Elizabeth Hodgkins, Marion E. Smart. *Not Fit For A Dog! The Truth About Manufactured Dog And Cat Food.*
Linden Publishing. 2008.

Martin, Ann. *Foods Pets Die For: Shocking Facts About Pet Food.* New Sage Press. 2008.

Parker-Pope, Tara. "Salmonella Lurks in Pet Foods Too," *The New York Times*, August 11, 2011.

Rodier, Lisa. "Carbs Contribute the Bulk of Your Dog's Kibble (Even Many Grain-Free Foods)," *Whole Dog Journal*, October 2010.

Storey, Samantha. "A Sniff of Home Cooking for Dogs and Cats," *The New York Times*, January 18, 2011.

Talley, Jessica Disbrow and Eric Talley.
The Organic Dog Biscuit Cookbook from the Bubba Rose's Biscuit Company.
Kennebunkport: Cider Mill Press, 2008.

Author Biography

arlotta Cooper was born and raised in Tennessee. Her grandparents were farmers, and she grew up with horses, dogs, and other animals. Her family raised chickens, ducks, geese, other poultry, rabbits, and pigs. She attended the University of the South in Sewanee where she graduated with a B.A. in English as class Salutatorian. She attended graduate school